D0943324

flaVored
Vinegars

To Margaux, Felicia, and Giana,
my three daughters, for their unrestrained love.

ACKNOWLEDGMENTS

When I think about all the people who deserve thanks
for their participation in my career, for listening to my dreams
and then pitching in to make them come true,
the list gets very, very long. I am glad to have the opportunity
to single out a few for special thanks.

To all the kitchen staff of TraVigne, and especially Michael
Gyetvan, Chef de Cuisine, and Carman Quagliata,
Dino DeBell, and Jim Humberd, Sous Chefs. They inspire me
daily with their unflagging passion for cooking.
They also keep me grounded with their gentle reminders
that whatever else I might be, underneath it all, I am a cook.

To my brother, Dr. Ronald Chiarello, for his very analytical
perspective on the chemistry of vinegar making.

To the team at Napa Valley Kitchens who have so successfully
launched the Vignette line of fruit-flavored vinegar
in 1994 and the Vignette savory vinegar line in 1995.

To John Foraker, President, for his calm confidence
and competence. He pulled us all together so that we could
take the tremendous strides necessary for the company's
health, well-being, and growth.

To Angela Gyetvan, Vice President of Marketing, for
her complete understanding of my dream and how to market it.

To Terry Dudley, Vice President of Sales, for his knowledge,
skill, and fresh, genuine enthusiasm.

To Karen Homick, manager of the Cantinetta and test cooking
assistant and guru. For her wry sense of humor as she
gathered all the ingredients and prepped each recipe while
assuring me that the many, many trays and bowls would all fit
in her VW bug for our trips to my house to test recipes.
Everything fit and she never forgot a thing!

To Michael Laukaurt, past manager of the Cantinetta and now
Research and Development Coordinator for Napa Valley
Kitchens. For his total dedication, belief, and loyalty as he spent
countless hours preparing and bottling my wacky vinegar ideas.

To Laura Chenel for introducing me to Dr. Moshé Shrifrine,
now the production chief of Napa Valley
Kitchens, and for sharing with me her dear friend, Penni.

To Nick Morfogen, my partner and the executive
chef of Ajax Tavern in Aspen, Colorado. For his numerous
vinegar ideas and for his love of cooking with them.

To Darrel Corti for his amazing knowledge of all that can be
consumed and for his generous sharing of that knowledge.

To Daniel Proctor, photographer, and Merilee Hague-Bordin,
stylist, for adding an entirely new dimension to my
books. It has been very exciting to see my work transformed
through Daniel's lens.

To my dear friend and cowriter, Penni Wisner, who makes
my passion for sharing my love of food and cooking a
tremendous joy. I am truly blessed to have crossed paths
with her. Thank you, Penni!

During the final editing of this book, our editor, Jackie Killeen
died of cancer. Jackie was a real professional; she knew
her stuff cold. She made the process of writing *Flavored Oils*
and this book so smooth even while she straightened
the most tangled mess of copy or a recipe. Jackie taught us a
great deal and she is very much missed.

flavored vinegars
50 Recipes for Cooking with infused vinegars
by Michael Chiarello
with Penelope Wisner
photography by Daniel Proctor

CHRONICLE BOOKS

SAN FRANCISCO

Text copyright
© 1996 by Michael Chiarello.

Photographs copyright
© 1996 by Daniel Proctor.

Design Calligraphy and Illustration copyright
© 1996 by Michael Mabry.

All rights reserved.
No part of this book may be
reproduced in any form
without written permission
from the publisher.

Library of Congress Cataloging in Publication Data:
Chiarello, Michael.
     Flavored vinegars: 50 recipes for cooking with infused vinegars / by
  Michael Chiarello, with Penelope Wisner; photography by Daniel Proctor.
        p. cm.
    Includes index.
    ISBN 0-8118-0872-6
    1. Cookery (Vinegar)   2. Vinegar.   I. Wisner, Penny. II. Title.
TX819.V5C45 1996
641.6′2—dc20   95-21547
                                    CIP

Book and Cover design by Michael Mabry
Food stylist: Merilee Hague-Bordin
Printed in Hong Kong.

Distributed in Canada
by Raincoast Books
8680 Cambie Street
Vancouver, B.C. V6P 6M9

10 9 8 7 6 5 4 3 2 1

Chronicle Books
275 Fifth Street
San Francisco, CA 94103

Contents

I do my best thinking while at the stove. As a chef, I am accustomed to letting the food I prepare "speak" for me. Writing books, however, forces me to think about what I am doing at the stove and why. Early in the process of writing this book, I was preparing a special harvest dinner for a large group in Napa Valley. As I stood at the stove finishing the second course, a pastina risotto, I thought about the day, the warmth of the room, and the rich flavors of the dish. Looking for harmony and balance, I added sherry vinegar to the sauce of reduced chicken stock, thyme, and sautéed garlic. Quite suddenly I understood why vinegar plays such an important role in my cooking! My cooking style emphasizes big flavors and using vinegar allows me to "turn up the volume" and still create dishes with harmony and balance. Vinegar as an ingredient, not just a condiment, acts in seemingly opposite ways: It generates a final effect of excitement and vibrancy by adding a layer of flavor underneath the other ingredients. The vinegar heightens and focuses all the flavors in the recipe.

Balance is key in cooking today and vinegar may be the most important tool in my *batterie de cuisine* for

achieving it. Food and dining have changed radically in the last ten years. We spend less time at table and serve fewer courses. Even this special dinner was only four courses. A few years ago, it might have been seven. So a cook has to work harder in each course to fill it with flavors and textures in order to give it the same impact as several courses of a dinner a decade ago.

Cooking is more fun and more soul satisfying when the cook has some involvement with the ingredients for a dish. Participation can be as basic as making your own vinegar or simply shopping carefully to find the best and most interesting vinegar to enhance your cooking style. By thinking ahead—taking advantage of seasonal ingredients or remembering to stop at a certain specialty shop—the work can be spread out to fit even the most compressed schedule.

In cooking—just as in selecting an exercise regimen—you have to choose the activities that speak to you and make you happy in the doing of them. If it is not making vinegar, then it might be making stock once a month to store in the freezer. Or it might be setting the table, or arranging the flowers, or choosing the wines or the music.

Making vinegar speaks to me because it is part of my family heritage. My mother made vinegar from wine that my father made. She made vinegar from all sorts of fruits as well, first fermenting their juice and then making vinegar.

When I started making vinegar at the restaurant, it was to extend this family heritage. The fruit vinegar came later, a surprising by-product of an experiment in preserving fruit for out-of-season use. A few years ago, we bought two hundred pounds of mangoes when they were tree-ripened and inexpensive. We had developed a mango sorbet for our dessert menu and wanted to be able to keep it once the mango season had passed. We hoped to purée and freeze the mangoes in order to keep them on hand. Unfortunately, the mangoes lost their vibrant, fresh flavor when frozen. With the help of my chemist brother, we acidified the purées so they would not ferment and began to use this vinegar-flavored fruit in pan sauces for duck and game, for vinaigrettes, marinades, and in desserts. We liked the idea so much we made a raspberry vinegar in the same way and have continued to experiment and develop new fruit vinegars. We bottled the mango vinegar first for sale in our Cantinetta. It was our customers who told us the vinegar made a great fat-free marinade and sauce all on its own.

When you are excited by the colors, aromas, tastes, and textures of your ingredients—and their potential to expand your repertoire of delicious, easily prepared dishes—you will want to cook! The recipes in this book will show you how easy it is to make a wine vinegar that will far surpass most of the commercial vinegars on the market. You will also be able to make herbal, fruit, and savory vinegars in a few minutes.

When it is time to cook with your vinegar, the ideas and techniques may be as simple as brushing fruit vinegar on fish or poultry before grilling or broiling. That the results taste so astoundingly good surprised even me! More time-consuming recipes are easily done ahead and even frozen. And when you do serve them, they will create such a stir, your guests—as our customers have—will ask for them again and again. My hope is that your success with these recipes will inspire you to cook more, and more often, and to spread the pleasure of good eating to all your family and friends.

We have taken vinegar for granted for so long, we have forgotten to wonder what it is and what its characteristics might be. We go to the grocery store and, without thinking, reach out for a bottle of cider vinegar for cooking or a large bottle of distilled vinegar for general household use and pickling.

If we left our habits at home and really looked at the shelves of vinegar in a well-stocked store, they would deliver a lesson in geography and anthropology. Vinegar comes from all over the world. The source materials for the vinegar, ranging from rice to barley, apples, and grapes, can tell us not only about the cuisine of the land of origin but about the staple crops of those countries. The cuisine of every country, it seems, depends in part on vinegar, and each has its own vinegar with particular characteristics: rice vinegar from China and Japan, malt vinegar from England, wine vinegar from France, sherry vinegar from Spain, balsamic vinegar from Italy. And there are variations on these—seasoned rice vinegar; herb, garlic, and fruit-flavored wine vinegar; lemon-flavored distilled vinegar.

All these choices represent only a small showing of the many types of vinegar made throughout history. Indeed, vinegar's history extends as far back as that of civilized man—one of the earliest written records mentioning vinegar dates from about 5000 BC.

All vinegar begins as a liquid containing alcohol. A certain bacteria of the genus Acetobacter is ever-present in the air and combines oxygen with alcohol to form acetic acid and water. Thus any liquid with enough sugar to support an alcoholic fermentation (caused by yeast) can become vinegar—and has. Historically, every civilization has made vinegar out of what was most commonly available: Ancient Babylonians made vinegar out of dates, while early Americans made vinegar out of apple cider. Asians used rice; Spanish, French, and Italians based their vinegar on wine.

Vinegar may be made from all sorts of fruits such as apples, pears, peaches, pineapples, grapes, persimmons, and berries; from grains including rice, barley, oats, and corn. The starch in grains must first be converted into sugar so that it can ferment. Vinegar may also be made from sweet syrups such as molasses, honey, and maple syrup as well as from distilled alcohol. Acetic acid gives vinegar its characteristic sour taste while the source material and aging regimens account for the different flavors and aromas of vinegar.

Vinegar making was probably discovered by accident, just as the first wines were. A jug of fresh fruit juice, such as grape juice, might have been left uncovered and unattended. Wild, airborne yeasts clinging to the grape skins or settling out of the air spontaneously began a primary alcoholic fermentation. Without effective means of preservation, the new wine quickly turned sour, to vinegar, through a secondary fermentation caused by acetobacters. Active acetobacters form a white veil on the surface of the liquid. This veil is called the vinegar "mother" and a piece of it can be used to quickly start vinegar fermentations. For commercial production, cultivated yeasts are added to the source material (such as grape juice) to start the primary fermentation and a vinegar "mother" is added to the new wine to give it a head start toward becoming vinegar and to beat out any other spoilage microorganisms.

The French, in particular, have excelled in vinegar production—with the exception, in my opinion, of the king of all vinegar, traditional balsamic vinegar. It was probably the French who first commercialized the production of vinegar and gave the sour liquid its name, *vin* (wine) and *aigre* (sour). They also developed the process for making high quality wine vinegar, the Orleans process. (See page 64-65 for a complete description of making vinegar by this process.) The French city, Orleans, lent its name to this method of vinegar production, which is still followed by home vinegar makers and commercial producers all over the world who want to make the best-tasting vinegar they can.

While the "hows" of vinegar making were widely understood and practiced all over the world for thousands of years, the "whys" were not understood until 1864 when Louis Pasteur demonstrated that acetobacters were responsible for the conversion of alcohol to acetic acid.

More than a century before Pasteur, a Dutch scientist, Hermann Boerhaave, discovered that increased aeration of the alcoholic liquid increased the rate of acetic acid production. To speed acetification and create less expensive vinegar, technologists, using Boerhaave's discovery, sought ways to increase the rate of aeration. In the twentieth century, continuous, commercial converters have been developed. These maintain an ideal warm temperature conducive to the growth of acetobacters and introduce a constant flow of air into the vinegar base. Modern converters can produce vinegar within twenty-four hours. The traditional Orleans process, while producing excellent tasting vinegar, requires a month or more. Orleans process vinegar is, therefore, relatively expensive.

OF GRAINS AND DEGREES:
The Strength of Vinegar

In theory, since acetic acid is produced through the action of acetobacters on alcohol in a dilute mixture, the more alcohol, the stronger the vinegar. This is not true in practice: Too high an alcohol content will kill the bacteria, while too low a concentration allows spoilage before turning the liquid to vinegar. Also, the acetic fermentation is not 100 percent "efficient"; evaporation and other causes will mean a lower conversion than theory would indicate.

Vinegar strength, the amount of acetic acid the liquid contains, is expressed as a percentage or in grains. The percentage is calculated as grams of acetic acid per 100 cubic centimeters. A grain is 0.1 gram of acid per 100 cubic centimeters of vinegar. A 4 percent vinegar could also be labeled as a 40 grain vinegar; a 5 percent vinegar, as a 50 grain vinegar.

Commercial vinegar must provide a consistent level of acetic acid. Government regulations insist that a liquid be 4 percent acetic acid in order to be labeled as vinegar. Commercial vinegar is typically thinned with water to provide a consistent strength. Check the label of any vinegar in your pantry to see how strong it is. American vinegars are usually 5 percent; imported wine vinegar is often 6 percent; rice vinegar is usually 4.3 percent; while the commercial vinegar I buy for my restaurants is 7 percent. If you use vinegar for pickling, I would advise using a commercial vinegar so you can depend on its strength.

The recipes in this book were tested with 6 percent vinegar—except the fruit and savory vinegar recipes. These latter are really fruit and vegetable purées flavored with vinegar. Their acetic strength is much less and they are not a substitute for vinegar but a new ingredient and condiment. Because people have different sensitivities to acid, it will be necessary to taste the dishes in this book and see if their balance suits your palate. Also make sure to read the label of the vinegar you choose to use: There will not be much appreciable difference between a 4 percent or 5 percent vinegar but there will be between a 4 percent and a 6 percent or 7 percent.

STORING VINEGAR

Store vinegar, either purchased or your own homemade vinegar, in nonreactive containers. Glass and ceramic are by far the best materials for containers. Metal and most plastic will react with vinegar over time and spoil both the container and the vinegar. I would not even recommend stainless steel: the high grade stainless steel necessary for long-term storage is very expensive!

Make sure the lids or stoppers you use are also nonreactive. Save corks from wine bottles to reuse or buy new ones from winemaking supply shops. Glass and ceramic stoppers are very good but are more expensive than cork. Well-stocked cookware and kitchen accessory shops often carry decorative bottles with ceramic stoppers. Another choice is an imported beer that comes in a dark brown, attractively decorated bottle with a ceramic stopper. It is good beer, and the bottle makes a terrific vinegar storage vessel that is good looking enough for a gift.

Beware of metal caps and lids, including canning lids. These will corrode. Some metal caps come lined with a thick paper pad. Make sure it is in place. You can line metal caps with plastic wrap or wax paper but use this only as a stopgap measure, as the vinegar will eventually eat through these as well.

For short-term storage of vinegar-based sauces such as vinaigrette and the fruit and savory vinegars in this book, glass jars with plastic lids saved from other foods work very well.

VINEGAR FROM AROUND THE WORLD

BALSAMIC VINEGAR: An aged wine vinegar made in the style of Modena, Italy. Intensely dark, powerfully aromatic, and tasting both sweet and tart, it is excellent for all sorts of cooking and can be used as a sauce on its own.

Prices vary as do quality and flavor from brand to brand. Choose a brand that is aged six or more years and preferably one from a good Italian producer.

TRADITIONAL BALSAMIC VINEGAR (*aceto balsamico tradizionale*): A unique wine vinegar, aged a minimum of twelve years in a series of barrels made of various kinds of wood. It is rare, expensive, and an absolute must-have for any serious cook. It is as spectacular as food can get. To be used by the drop.

CHAMPAGNE VINEGAR: Wine vinegar made from champagne stock (fermented champagne grapes before they undergo the second fermentation that gives the wine its bubbles). Since grapes picked for champagne or sparkling wine are picked at lower degrees of ripeness than those for still wines, champagne vinegar should have a delicate, clean acid taste. It may also have a lower acidity than other wine vinegars unless it has been corrected by the producer. Use champagne vinegar for vinaigrettes, and, because of its delicate character, as a base for herb and fruit-flavored vinegar.

CIDER VINEGAR: The traditional, all-American vinegar made from apple cider. It can be used as an all-purpose cooking vinegar, lends its fruitiness well to salad dressings, and can work as a substitute for rice vinegar.

DISTILLED VINEGAR: A crystal-clear vinegar made from dilute distilled alcohol. Good for pickling and a necessity for general household use.

FRUIT VINEGAR: Commercial fruit vinegars are usually made by macerating whole fruit in white wine or champagne vinegar. After the flavor and color has infused the vinegar, the solids are filtered out. The strength varies by brand and is usually 5 percent or 6 percent acetic acid. The vinegars have more or less fruit aroma and flavor, again, depending on the brand. These vinegars are appropriate for vinaigrettes and pan sauces. Fruit vinegars (cider vinegar, see above, is a classic example) made from whole fruit which is crushed, fermented to produce alcohol, then fermented again with acetobacter bacteria to produce acetic acid, may also sometimes be found. These, such as pear vinegar or pineapple vinegar, are well worth trying if you come across them. The fruit vinegars in this book do *not* fit this description at all and the various types do not substitute for each other easily. Fruit vinegars as described in this book are fruit purées flavored with vanilla and vinegar. They have intense, fresh fruit flavors, a thick texture, and a much lower acetic acid content than most commercial fruit vinegars. My own brand, Consorzio, and our Vignette line are in this fruit-flavored-vinegar style.

MALT VINEGAR: Made from the fermented mash of malted barley (much like beer). Malt vinegar is the national vinegar of England where it is the condiment for fish and chips. It is also made in Germany and other countries with a strong beer-making tradition. It is often used for pickling and is an ingredient in Worcestershire sauce.

RICE VINEGAR: Once made from rice and now usually made from rice wine lees. It is usually slightly sweet and mild and 4.3 percent acidity. Rice vinegar is made in both China and Japan.

SHERRY VINEGAR: Made from sherry wine, this is the traditional vinegar of Spain. It is a medium brown color with the lovely, rich wood and nut scents typical of sherry. Its full body and slightly sweet taste give it a starring role in dressings for substantial salads including meat, poultry, cheese, and/or fruit. Its flavors allow it to blend particularly well with nut oils.

WINE VINEGAR: Made from both red and white wine. Red wine vinegar makes great mustard vinaigrettes and for braising meat such as beef and game. White wine vinegar may sometimes be harsh, so look for a high quality brand. Use white wine vinegar as you would champagne vinegar. Use both red and white wine vinegar for making flavored vinegar; use the red for robust blends of herbs and spices and the white for more delicate herbs.

VINEGAR AND PROTEIN

Vinegar "cooks" (denatures) protein. In the restaurant, we call it cold cooking. This is the secret of ceviche, the Mexican raw fish salad. The fish sits in a lemon juice mixture until it is "cooked." You have to be careful when marinating fish: The marinade should not be strongly acid and the fish should not marinate long or it will over-cook and dry out instead of just absorbing flavor.

The denaturing of protein is also the secret behind perfect poached eggs. Putting vinegar in the poaching water will help the whites hold around the yolks.

Vinegar also helps the cook make perfect emulsified sauces with eggs. When vinegar is added to the mixture, the temperature at which egg protein coagulates rises to 195° F instead of the normal 160° F, allowing for a more stable sauce.

Once upon a time, every American housewife made her own vinegar. She began with whatever fruit was ripe and abundant, most frequently apples. If she were very economical, she made vinegar from the fruit parings and cores. She fermented the fruit to make hard apple cider, then covered the jug with cloth to keep out flies and dust, and waited. If she had an active vinegar mother (the whitish veil composed of acetobacters that grows on the surface of vinegar-in-the-making), or had a piece from a neighbor, she would add it as soon as the cider had finished its alcoholic fermentation. (Having a mother starts the vinegar fermentation more rapidly.) After a few weeks, airborne bacteria would have begun a second fermentation in the jug—from cider to vinegar. The housewife would taste the new vinegar over a period of weeks and months. When it was strong enough to suit her taste, she poured it into bottles and corked them.

My method for making fruit vinegar was born out of a failure, as discoveries often are. I was working with mangoes and meant to purée and freeze them so I would have them on hand when needed. Unfortunately, I felt freezing ruined their flavor. In order to prevent two hundred pounds of fruit from going bad, I preserved it with vinegar, and only then discovered how good it tasted and how much fun I could have with it in the kitchen!

The fruit vinegar technique described here takes only a few minutes and begins with very aromatic, ripe fruit that is not too watery. Just about any fruit you can buy can be turned into a fruit vinegar. My preference is for tropical fruits such as mango, guava, passion fruit, and coconut. Apples, pears, peaches, and strawberries are less intense in flavor because of their high water content. Their flavors are more delicate than the tropical fruits and the vinegar appears to destroy a good deal of the fruit flavor. On the other hand, raspberries and other berries, in particular wild berries that are often starved for water, make fabulous vinegar with this method.

The technique produces a product not immediately recognizable as vinegar. It is more comparable to a flavored fruit purée. The taste—both sweet and lightly tart—and texture of these fruit vinegars give them all sorts of culinary uses you might not ordinarily think of when thinking about vinegar.

● Use for fruit juice drinks such as freshly squeezed orange juice and fruit vinegar. Experiment with combinations of different juices and vinegar.

● Make spritzers: pour 1 tablespoon fruit vinegar in a glass, add ice and carbonated water, and stir. The sweet fruitiness makes these spritzers delicious and the vinegar makes them very refreshing.

● Add an exotic touch to all sorts of salsas. Splash a tablespoon or two of fruit vinegar into your favorite salsa or create new ones such as a carrot salsa with red pepper, chili, cilantro, and fruit vinegar. Black beans and rice is a whole new dish topped with a fruit salsa including banana, avocado, mango, papaya, cilantro, onion, jalapeño, and fruit vinegar.

● Tropical fruit vinegar tastes wonderful with herbs, especially basil, mint, and rosemary. Blend the vinegar with flavored oils or with freshly chopped herbs and olive oil as dressings for lettuce and vegetable salads.

● Use fruit vinegars in desserts! They taste great poured straight on vanilla ice cream, or to make a fruit salad, or as a sauce for pound cake.

● Make a dessert butter sauce by gently melting butter, then whisking in fruit vinegar. Do not overheat or the butter will separate. Thin with heavy cream.

● Give caramel sauces a whole range of new flavors by adding fruit vinegar. Make your caramel with sugar and water and add cream, if using. Stir in the fruit vinegar last to keep the flavor as fresh and vibrant as possible.

● *Caution:* When making vinaigrettes with fruit vinegar, use light-tasting oils such as French or Spanish extra-virgin olive oil or regular olive oil, or vegetable oil. The richer, more pronounced flavor of Italian and Californian extra-virgin olive oil is too powerful to complement fruit vinegar.

● *Note:* Do not subject fruit vinegars to high heat such as grilling over a hot fire. The natural fruit sugars as well as the added sugar makes them susceptible to burning.

MAKING FRUIT VINEGAR

The basic components are very simple: a vanilla-scented sugar syrup (see recipe following), fruit, 6 percent champagne vinegar, and salt. The salt brings out the fruit flavor. You can use fresh or frozen fruit to make fruit vinegar. Raspberry, mango, and cranberry are particular favorites. I have never been successful with blueberry. I think its high pectin content does not lend itself well to this method.

Harder fruits such as pears and apples can be cooked in the vanilla syrup until they cook to a loose purée. Then blend with a pinch of salt and strain. The flavor of some fruit—peaches, for instance—intensifies with cooking. These, too, can be cooked in the syrup in order to make a vinegar. Experiment by making small batches with both methods—puréeing and cooking—for other fruits and combinations of fruits.

You will need to taste your vinegar for balance; it is impossible to predict the sweetness of fresh fruit in season and the different brands of frozen fruit. Use the amount of syrup given because it adds body to the mixture. If you want your vinegar to taste more tart than your result with these proportions, add a little more vinegar. If your vinegar is too thick, thin with water.

Try to make your fruit vinegar a day ahead of time. All fruit vinegars seem to go through a "flavor shock" when first made. The fruit flavor gets stronger the next day.

Fruit vinegar will keep several weeks, refrigerated, but the flavor will be best within the first week. Be sure to store in glass or ceramic containers sealed with non-metallic lids.

VANILLA-SCENTED SUGAR SYRUP

Keep this syrup on hand to add to iced tea and other cold drinks or for poaching fruit. It does not need to be refrigerated. The vanilla is minced to make sure all its flavor is extracted into the syrup.

4   cups sugar
1   cup water
2   vanilla beans, minced,
       or 2 tablespoons pure vanilla extract

Put the sugar, water, and vanilla beans (if using) in a pot and bring to a boil over high heat. Lower heat to a simmer and cook about 4 minutes. Stir occasionally. Let cool. Purée syrup in a blender until vanilla beans are thoroughly chopped into the syrup. Strain through a fine strainer into a jar. If using vanilla extract instead of beans, add extract after the sugar syrup has cooled and pour into a jar. Seal tightly.

Makes about 3¼ cups.

RASPBERRY VINEGAR

This makes an intensely red-garnet colored vinegar. Use it for duck and chicken as well as asparagus or green beans. Raspberries have a special affinity for nuts, especially hazelnuts. If using fresh fruit, be sure to taste as you go to adjust syrup to the sweetness of the berries. The vinegar should taste of berries and be sweet with the clean, vinegar flavor lingering in the mouth.

½ pint ripe raspberries
½ cup vanilla-scented sugar syrup (page 16)
   Pinch salt
¼ cup champagne vinegar (6 percent acidity)

Purée berries, sugar syrup, and salt together in a blender. Add vinegar and taste for balance. Add more vinegar and thin with water if necessary. Strain through a fine strainer into a bowl or pitcher. Store in a clean jar or bottle (do not use metal lids or tops) and refrigerate.

Makes about 1 cup.

Variation with Frozen Raspberries: Use one 12-ounce bag frozen, unsweetened raspberries, ¾ cup vanilla-scented sugar syrup, pinch salt, and ½ cup champagne vinegar (6 percent acidity).

Makes about 2¼ cups.

MANGO VINEGAR

Mango is probably the most popular fruit vinegar of my vinegar line. It has a wonderful aroma. Pour it over ice cream—and add chopped ginger in syrup or crystallized ginger and perhaps crumbled gingersnaps.

2 large, ripe mangoes, peeled and cut into ½-inch dice (about 2½ cups)
½ cup vanilla-scented sugar syrup (page 16)
   Pinch salt
½ cup champagne vinegar (6 percent acidity)

Purée mangoes, sugar syrup, and salt together in a blender. Add vinegar and taste for balance. Add more vinegar and thin with water if necessary. Strain through a fine strainer into a bowl or pitcher. Store in a clean jar or bottle (do not use metal lids or tops) and refrigerate.

Makes about 2½ cups.

CRANBERRY VINEGAR

Try this vinegar instead of cranberry sauce for your next holiday bird. Cranberries freeze without loss of flavor so don't let frozen berries stop you from making this vinegar!

1 bag (12 ounces) fresh or frozen cranberries
¼ cup vanilla-scented sugar syrup (page 16)
   Pinch salt
¾ cup champagne vinegar (6 percent acidity)

Put cranberries, syrup, and salt in a pan and heat over high heat until cranberries begin to pop. Remove from heat, let cool, then purée in a blender. Add vinegar and taste for balance. Add more vinegar and thin with water if necessary. Strain through a fine strainer into a bowl or pitcher. Store in a clean jar or bottle (do not use metal lids or tops) and refrigerate. Keeps several weeks.

Makes about 3 cups.

This recipe belongs to my wife. We met at the Culinary Institute of America in Hyde Park, New York, where we both were students. The recipe, as given by the school, called for equal parts soy sauce, ketchup, and honey. Ines has changed it a great deal since then and uses it often at home on ribs, chicken, and shrimp. When we started making our fruit vinegar, her sauce changed again to incorporate the new taste.

¾	cup dark soy sauce
1	cup ketchup
1	tablespoon finely chopped garlic
1	tablespoon finely grated fresh ginger
1	cup honey
½	cup mango vinegar (page 17)

Whisk soy sauce, ketchup, garlic, ginger, honey, and vinegar together in a bowl or large jar. Cover tightly with a nonmetallic lid and refrigerate. Use as you would any barbecue sauce. (See Chef's Notes for ideas.) Do not use very high heat with this sauce or it may burn. Keeps several weeks.

Makes about 3 cups.

CHEF'S NOTES: *Ribs and chicken pieces can be marinated in sauce overnight, drained, then basted with sauce during cooking. For ribs, start them in a preheated 300°F oven for 1 hour, lower heat to 250°F for another 2 hours. You can also dispense with marinating whole chickens or chicken pieces ahead of time and simply brush them with sauce before cooking, then baste often. For shrimp, dip them in sauce, then grill over medium heat. Once done, sprinkle with finely sliced green onions (green part only), a tablespoon or so sesame oil and, if you want to add some heat, flavored olive oil using dried and/or fresh hot chilies, sweet bell peppers, and peppercorns (see Glossary).*

This is a charming soup with a surprisingly sophisticated flavor. The basil and pine nuts add depth and texture to this very pretty, pink soup. Since its success depends entirely on the quality of the fruit used, I would not advise making this soup off season. The berries must be ripe and full of flavor. The sweetness can be adjusted by adding more or less sugar or honey depending on the flavor of the fruit used. Serve the soup as a first course or for a luncheon with a salad.

4	baskets raspberries (½ pint each)
⅓	cup grappa or light rum
1	cup heavy cream
1	tablespoon sugar or to taste
1	tablespoon honey or to taste
	Pinch salt
2	tablespoons finely chopped fresh basil
1	teaspoon raspberry vinegar (page 17)
1	tablespoon toasted pine nuts (see Glossary)
2	tablespoons mascarpone cheese (optional)

Reserve several berries for garnish and purée the rest in a food processor or blender. With machine running, add rum and blend well. Add cream, sugar, honey, and salt. Pulse in half the basil. Pour into a bowl, cover, and refrigerate until ready to serve.

Pour the soup into 4 bowls and sprinkle ¼ teaspoon raspberry vinegar onto each. The vinegar will form pretty red droplets on the surface. Garnish with pine nuts, reserved berries, remaining basil, and a dollop of mascarpone, if desired.

Serves 4.

Variation with Strawberries and Peaches: Use 1 pint strawberries and 4 fresh peaches (peeled, pitted, and sliced) instead of the raspberries. Use fresh mint instead of basil.

A light sweetness from the binding of mascarpone cheese and the topping of grape relish makes this an unusual pasta. Serve it in small portions as a first course and follow it with something very simple such as a roast chicken. Or serve it as a supper dish with a salad of bitter greens such as baby spinach or arugula.

	Salt and freshly ground pepper
1	pound dried pastina pasta (Acini di Pepe from De Cecco)
4	tablespoons extra-virgin olive oil
¼	cup raisins
1	teaspoon minced shallot
1	teaspoon minced fresh rosemary
2–4	tablespoons cranberry vinegar (page 17)
1	cup halved seedless grapes
1	tablespoon finely chopped garlic
2	tablespoons minced fresh sage or 2 teaspoons dried sage
1¼	cups roasted chicken stock (see next page) or low-salt, canned chicken broth
½	cup mascarpone cheese
½	cup freshly grated Parmesan cheese
2	tablespoons finely chopped fresh flat-leaf parsley
1¼	ounces thinly sliced prosciutto, cut into thin strips

Bring a large pot of salted water to a boil and add pastina. Stir often to prevent it from sticking to the bottom of the pan and cook until tender, about 15 minutes. Drain, toss with 2 tablespoons olive oil, and reserve.

Put the raisins in a small bowl and add warm water to cover. Let sit 15 minutes to soften and plump. Drain and replace in bowl with shallots, rosemary, 2 tablespoons cranberry vinegar, and grapes. Mix well and set aside.

In a large, deep sauté pan, heat remaining 2 tablespoons oil over medium-high heat until almost smoking. Add garlic and sauté quickly until lightly browned, moving the pan off and on heat to regulate temperature. Add sage, then stock, and bring to a boil. Boil until reduced by ¼. Season to taste with salt and pepper. Add reserved pastina and cook until pastina has absorbed most of the liquid and pan is almost dry. (If you do not have a pan large enough to hold all the pasta, return drained, oiled pasta to pasta pot and pour sauce over it.) Remove from heat and add mascarpone cheese. Stir well until mascarpone has melted and blended in. Add Parmesan and 1 tablespoon parsley. Toss well. Divide among 4 to 6 hot plates and top each with grape relish, prosciutto, and a sprinkling of the remaining 1 tablespoon parsley.

Serves 4 to 6

ROASTED CHICKEN STOCK

I like to use a roasted chicken stock in the winter for its dark color, and rich, caramelized flavors. When spring comes again, I switch back to a blond chicken stock for most dishes. Make sure to roast the bones well and to brown the vegetables for maximum flavor. However, use whatever stock (roasted or blond, homemade or canned) you have on hand. Chicken stock is such an important ingredient, its quality will have a huge impact on your cooking. I encourage you to get in the habit of making a batch once a month or seeking out a very good quality canned broth. It is also possible to convince your favorite restaurant to sell you some of theirs.

5	pounds chicken bones
2	tablespoons extra-virgin olive oil (optional)
1	large onion, cut into 1-inch chunks
2	carrots, cut into 1-inch chunks
2	stalks celery, cut into 1-inch chunks
1	cup dry red wine
10	cups cold water
1	bay leaf
10	peppercorns
5	juniper berries

Preheat oven to 450°F. Place bones in a roasting pan or baking sheet with sides and place in the oven. Roast until browned all over, about 1 hour. Make sure to stir bones occasionally so they brown evenly.

While bones are roasting, heat olive oil in a stockpot over medium-high heat until almost smoking. (Or use some chicken fat from the roasting bones.) Add onion, carrot, and celery and sauté over medium heat until richly browned, about 15 minutes. Add red wine and stir well, making sure to scrape up any browned bits from the sides and bottom of the pan.

Add bones and cold water and bring to a boil over high heat. Reduce heat to a simmer and add bay leaf, peppercorns, and juniper berries. Skim frequently for the first hour and continue to simmer slowly, uncovered, another 4 hours, skimming occasionally. Strain, cool, and refrigerate. When fat has congealed, lift it off and discard. Cover and refrigerate or freeze.

Makes about 5 cups.

Variation for Blond Chicken Stock: Rinse bones with cold water, then put in a pot and cover with cold water. Let rest 10 minutes, then drain and rinse again. This washes off the blood and allows a clearer stock. Return chicken bones to pot and add water. Bring to a boil, reduce heat, and simmer 30 minutes. Skim foam frequently. Continue to skim until mixture stops foaming. Add onions, carrots, celery, bay leaves, peppercorns, and juniper berries and continue as above.

SPICY TROPICAL FRUIT SALSA

Serve this easy salsa with shrimp adobo, grilled chicken, Hawaiian fish such as ahi; as the dipping sauce for shrimp cocktail; with broiled lobster; and even as a garnish for raw oysters. In summer, when peaches and nectarines are ripe, use them instead of mangoes or papayas.

1	cup cut-up pineapple (¼-inch cubes)
1	cup cut-up mango (¼-inch cubes)
1	cup cut-up papaya (¼-inch cubes)
2	serrano chilies, roasted, peeled, seeded, and finely minced (see Chef's Notes)
1	tablespoon minced red onion
½	teaspoon finely grated ginger
½	cup mango vinegar (page 17)
	Salt and freshly ground pepper
1	tablespoon finely chopped fresh cilantro
1	tablespoon toasted pine nuts (see Glossary)

Mix together all ingredients in a nonreactive bowl. Cover with a nonmetallic lid such as plastic wrap and refrigerate at least 1 hour before serving. Keeps about 2 days before texture of fruit begins to deteriorate.

Makes about 3 cups.

CHEF'S NOTES: *Taste a tiny bite of the serrano on bread before adding it to the salsa. Some are very hot; others not very. By tasting first, you can adjust the heat of the salsa to your preference. To roast serranos, I place them in a small pan in very hot olive oil. Brown on all sides in the pan, then let cool. Peel off and discard the dark skin and interior seeds.*

GRILLED CHICKEN MARINATED IN MANGO VINEGAR AND TARRAGON

Mango vinegar by itself works amazingly well as a marinade for roasted, baked, or grilled poultry. Serve the chicken with jasmine rice and thin green beans with roasted walnuts. For a simple salad, tear the chicken into pieces and toss with baby greens and a vinaigrette of mango vinegar and olive oil. Or make a chicken salad sandwich by adding diced celery and onion to the chicken and binding with mayonnaise mixed with a little mango vinegar for extra flavor.

4	skinless, boneless chicken breast halves
½	cup mango vinegar (page 17)
2	teaspoons finely chopped fresh tarragon or 1 teaspoon dried tarragon
	Salt and freshly ground pepper

Prepare grill or preheat broiler. Put chicken in a bowl and pour mango vinegar over it. Add tarragon and turn breasts until well coated.

Oil grill or broiler rack. Season chicken on both sides with salt and pepper and cook over medium heat with no flame. If the fire is too hot, the sugar in the vinegar will burn instead of caramelize. Grill on one side until brown, about 5 minutes. Turn and baste with mango vinegar. Continue to cook until done, about 5 minutes more. Pass more vinegar at table as a sauce.

Serves 4.

Even if I do say so myself, these figs are insanely good. Serve them without salad as an hors d'oeuvre at cocktail parties. When figs are out of season, use pears, apples, or Japanese Fuju persimmons, all cut into large pieces. Use the dressing on asparagus, green beans, baby spinach, or chard. Do not use extra-virgin olive oil in the dressing; its flavor will overpower the raspberry flavor.

¼	cup hazelnuts
¼	cup plus 1 tablespoon raspberry vinegar (page 17)
	Salt and freshly ground pepper
2	tablespoons olive oil or flavored olive oil using lavender (see Glossary)
12	fresh figs (ripe but firm), stems removed and halved
1½	ounces pancetta (see Glossary), cut into paper-thin slices about 4 inches long
4	cups (about ¼ pound) mixed salad greens such as a mesclun mix

Preheat oven to 350°F and toast hazelnuts until fragrant and lightly browned, about 10 minutes. Remove and wrap in a kitchen towel. Let rest a few minutes, then vigorously rub the nuts against each other inside the towel to rub off their skins. Roughly chop a few of the nuts to make about 1 tablespoon for garnish and reserve. Place the remaining nuts in a blender or small food processor and process until finely ground. Continue to process until the nuts turn into a paste. You should have about 2 tablespoons paste. With machine running, add ¼ cup vinegar and salt and pepper and process until mixture is smooth. Again, with machine running, add oil slowly so mixture forms an emulsion.

Preheat grill. Wrap each fig half in a slice of pancetta. Stretch pancetta as you work so it sticks tightly to the fruit. The slices will adhere to themselves and not need a skewer. Place figs over a hot grill and cook quickly, turning to cook all sides, until pancetta is crisp but fig remains slightly cool, about 3 minutes.

To serve, toss greens in a bowl with about 2 tablespoons hazelnut dressing. Arrange ¼ of the greens on each of 4 plates. Top with several figs and drizzle remaining dressing over them. Sprinkle plates with reserved nuts and remaining 1 tablespoon raspberry vinegar.

Serves 4.

CHEF'S NOTES: *If you want to cut down on fat a little, wrap pancetta around the fruit only once instead of twice. In that case, you will need only half the listed weight of pancetta.*

If you do not have a blender or small food processor, it might be easier to double the amount of hazelnuts and other dressing ingredients. It keeps, refrigerated, at least several weeks.

It was lunchtime for the restaurant kitchen staff. My sous chef and I wanted pizza but knew we should have some salad. We didn't have time for both. Inspiration hit: We stacked salad on top of a freshly baked pizza, folded it in half, and ate standing up, leaning over the counter. I think we made different versions of pizza sandwiches for our lunch every day that summer. The dish is not on our menu, but friends and guests who have been introduced to it often request it. One of my favorite pizza sandwiches is stuffed with roasted garlic Caesar salad.

¾	pound squid or rock shrimp, cleaned
5	tablespoons flavored olive oil using dried hot chilies, sweet bell peppers, and peppercorns (see Glossary)
	Salt and freshly ground pepper
2	tablespoons extra-virgin olive oil
2	tablespoons thinly sliced garlic
2	cups thinly sliced yellow onion (see Chef's Notes)
1	cup water
1	tablespoon finely chopped fresh thyme
2	bunches green onions (white part only), thinly sliced
1	recipe pizza dough (see Glossary)
	Coarse cornmeal for sprinkling on baking sheets
8	cups mixed baby salad greens
3	tablespoons mango vinegar (page 17)
2	tablespoons finely chopped fresh flat-leaf parsley

Preheat grill or broiler. Put squid in a bowl and pour 2 tablespoons pepper oil over it. Toss well and marinate a few minutes while grill is preheating. Season with salt and pepper, then place squid directly on an oiled grill above the coals. Cook squid until just done: It will begin to roll up and the flesh will no longer be translucent, about 3 minutes. Do not overcook or squid will be tough. Let cool and cut bodies and tentacles into ¼-inch-thick pieces. Reserve.

Heat extra-virgin olive oil in a large sauté pan over medium-high heat until almost smoking. Add garlic and sauté, moving pan off and on heat to regulate temperature, until lightly brown. Add yellow onion and lower heat to medium. Season with salt and pepper. Sauté until onion wilts, about 3 minutes. Add water, cover, and steam 5 minutes. Uncover and add thyme. Stir and cook until pan is almost dry. Add green onions and cook until wilted.

Preheat oven to 500°F. Place baking sheets in oven to preheat. Divide pizza dough into 3 portions and shape each into a circle about 10 inches in diameter and about ⅛ inch thick. Remove pans from oven, sprinkle with cornmeal, and transfer pizzas to baking sheets. Brush each pizza with about 1 teaspoon pepper oil. Spread equal amounts of onion mixture on each. Make sure to spread mixture within ½ inch of border all the way around. Place in oven and bake until lightly brown, about 10 minutes. Pizza should be cooked but still flexible.

While pizzas are baking, place squid and salad greens in a bowl and toss with vinegar and remaining 2 tablespoons pepper oil. Season with salt and pepper and add parsley. Toss well. Immediately pile freshly baked pizzas with salad mix, fold pizza in half over the salad, cut in half at a 90-degree angle to the fold, and serve.

Makes 3 large pizza sandwiches; serves 6.

CHEF'S NOTES: *Cut the onions as you would for French onion soup: First cut the onion in half lengthwise, then slice each half lengthwise into ¼-inch-thick slices.*

TORTA SABIOSA
FLOURLESS "POUND" CAKE

This is a traditional Italian cake from the Po River valley, famous for its potatoes and rice. Potato starch is a by-product of potato processing so it is used frequently in the cuisine of the area. Sabiosa means sandlike and the cake has such a delicate, light texture it seems to melt away in the mouth. The cake may also be made in muffin tins lined with muffin papers. Sabiosa makes a terrific tiramisu (the Italian dessert) or use it instead of a shortcake to make berry shortcakes. This recipe was given to me by Marta Pulini, chef of Mad 61 in New York City, who is a native of Modena and an expert on the foods of the Po River valley.

	Butter and flour for preparing cake pans
2	sticks (½ pound) unsalted butter at room temperature
1	cup plus 1 tablespoon superfine sugar
2	eggs, separated
2	tablespoons grated lemon zest
½	teaspoon pure vanilla extract
1½	teaspoons brandy or more vanilla extract
1⅓	cups potato starch, sifted after measuring
1½	teaspoons baking powder

Put rack in center of oven and preheat oven to 350°F. Prepare 1 round cake pan (9 x 2 inches deep) by buttering and flouring bottom and sides, then lining bottom with baking parchment or waxed paper.

Put butter in the bowl of an electric mixer and beat at medium speed with paddle attachment until light and fluffy, about 5 minutes. Add 1 cup sugar and beat well again until very fluffy. Add egg yolks, one at a time, beating well at medium or medium-high speed, after each. Beat in lemon zest, vanilla, and brandy. Then quickly stir in potato starch and baking powder.

In another bowl, with clean beaters, beat egg whites with remaining 1 tablespoon sugar until soft peaks form. Add ½ of whites to potato starch mixture and gently mix with a wide rubber spatula to lighten batter. Scrape rest of egg whites into batter and fold gently until whites are incorporated. Do not overmix or batter will deflate.

Scrape batter into prepared cake pan and level with the spatula. Bake in the preheated oven 45 minutes or until a cake tester comes out clean. Let cake cool in pan on a rack. Cut around sides and turn out, then peel off paper. Wrap well and refrigerate if not using immediately. The cake does not need icing, simply cut into wedges and serve with lampone pazzo (page 27).

Makes one 9-inch cake.

CHEF'S NOTE: *This cake is so delicate it will go stale rapidly. Make it as close to serving time as possible or make sure to wrap very well and refrigerate. Bring to room temperature before serving.*

Recipe may be doubled. Use three 9 x 1½-inch round cake pans. (The recipe as is makes a little too much batter for a standard depth cake pan. This extra batter, when the recipe is doubled, converts to a third layer in standard pans.) Increase potato starch to 2¾ cups.

Serve these berries with biscotti and a dollop of mascarpone cheese or whipped cream. For a pretty presentation, crumble the biscotti into a wine glass and top with the fruit. Lampone pazzo are also delicious on top of vanilla gelato, with panna cotta (literally, "cooked cream," an Italian dessert made of cream thickened and stabilized with gelatin), with toasted polenta pound cake, or the powder-puff light cake, sabiosa (page 25). You can also use strawberries, blueberries, or just about any berry you like that is in season.

2	cups fresh raspberries
½	cup superfine sugar
6	tablespoons raspberry vinegar (page 17)
	Pinch salt and freshly ground black pepper
	One 9-inch or 6 individual sabiosa cakes (recipe follows)
	Sweetened whipped cream or mascarpone cheese for garnish

Combine raspberries, sugar, vinegar, salt, and pepper in a nonreactive bowl and let marinate on the counter 5 to 10 minutes. Cut sabiosa into wedges and place one on each of 6 plates. Pile berries on top and garnish with a dollop of whipped cream or mascarpone.

Layered Variation: For a festive presentation, use 2 layers of sabiosa. Reserve about 2 tablespoons of fresh berries before mixing them with the vinegar. Place one sabiosa layer on a cake plate. Pile the lampone pazzo on the layer as a filling. Top with second layer and spread top of it with sweetened whipped cream or mascarpone. Garnish with fresh berries.

This is probably the simplest recipe in the book and it is packed with flavor. A granita is a sweetened mixture (often fruit juice or espresso) without enrichments such as eggs or cream, frozen until hard in a flat dish or ice cube tray, then scraped with a fork into crystals or flakes and spooned into dessert glasses. Serve this granita as a light dessert after a rich meal with perhaps chocolate-coated biscotti on the side, or, more spectacularly, with a warm chocolate cake! You can have fun with presentation by lining the pan with parchment paper and cutting the granita into shapes such as triangles instead of just spooning it into a glass. The granita may also be made with raspberry purée and raspberry vinegar.

4	cups mango purée made from fresh, ripe mangoes, about 5 large mangoes (see Chef's Notes)
¾	cup mango vinegar (page 17)
	Pinch salt

Mix together all ingredients in a bowl. Pour into a shallow pan and place in the freezer until hard. When ready to serve, shave granita into small glass dishes and serve immediately.

Serves 6.

CHEF'S NOTES: *Make sure the fruit is very ripe and sweet. If sugar needs to be added, the balance and texture will change. If your purée is full of strings, strain before mixing with vinegar.*

PEACH AND BOYSENBERRY COBBLER

Like crisps, a cobbler needs no embellishments because the taste of fresh, ripe fruit is the point of this dessert. Use whatever fruit is in the height of its season. On the cusp of fall, for instance, I mix peaches with quince and will often add red bananas for their richness and subtle tropical flavor. Cut the extra dough into strips, roll up into spirals, and sprinkle or roll in cinnamon sugar as a treat for the kids.

FRUIT MIXTURE

6	large, ripe peaches, peeled, pitted, and cut into ¼-inch slices (about 5 cups)
3	tablespoons quick-cooking tapioca
5	tablespoons granulated sugar
	Pinch salt
1½	cups boysenberries or raspberries
2–3	tablespoons mango vinegar (page 17)

PASTRY AND TOPPINGS

2	cups all-purpose flour plus more for dusting work surface
½	teaspoon salt
4	tablespoons firmly packed light or dark brown sugar
2	teaspoons baking powder
¾	stick (6 tablespoons) cold unsalted butter, broken or cut into small pieces
1¾	cups plus 1 tablespoon heavy cream
¼	cup granulated sugar
½	teaspoon pure vanilla extract

Preheat oven to 350°F. In a large bowl, combine peaches, tapioca, granulated sugar, and salt. Gently mix in berries and 2 tablespoons vinegar. Taste for balance and add more vinegar, if desired. Spoon mixture into an 8 x 8-inch ovenproof baking dish.

Combine flour, salt, 3 tablespoons brown sugar, and baking powder in a mixing bowl. Cut in butter until mixture forms balls the size of large peas. This can be done with the paddle attachment of a stand mixer, with brief pulses of a food processor, or by hand with a pastry blender. Slowly mix in ¾ cup heavy cream until just combined.

Gather dough together into a ball and knead gently on a lightly floured board until it holds together. Roll out until ½ inch thick. Using a 3-inch round or star cutter, cut dough into shapes. Place them on top of peach mixture. Brush pastry with 1 tablespoon cream. Sprinkle with remaining 1 tablespoon brown sugar. Bake in the preheated oven until pastry is golden brown, about 40 minutes. Put cobbler under broiler for a few seconds to brown pastry if necessary.

Beat remaining scant cup cream in a small bowl with a whisk or electric mixer. When it begins to foam, add ¼ cup granulated sugar by small spoonfuls. Beat until it holds soft peaks, then beat in vanilla. Serve with cobbler.

Serves 6 to 8.

Upside-down cakes are an old-fashioned American dessert. In summer, use ripe peaches and nectarines, even plums. The cake is uncomplicated and not very sweet by itself; the pineapple juices and brown sugar sauce permeate the cake as it bakes. The result is luscious.

1½	sticks (¾ cup) unsalted butter, at room temperature plus more for baking pan
½	cup plus 1 tablespoon superfine sugar plus more for dusting baking pan
2	large eggs, separated
1½	cups all-purpose flour
2	teaspoons baking powder
	Pinch salt
1	cup milk
¼	cup mango vinegar (page 17)
½	cup packed light or dark brown sugar (see Chef's Notes)
6	fresh pineapple rings, peeled, cored, and cut ½ inch thick
¼	cup toasted, roughly chopped macadamia nuts (see Glossary)

Preheat oven to 350°F. Butter and sugar a 9 x 2-inch round baking pan or 6 ramekins (4-inch diameter). Put 1 stick softened butter in the bowl of an electric mixer. Beat on medium to high speed with the paddle attachment until light and fluffy. Add ½ cup superfine sugar and beat very well, until mixture is white and very light and fluffy. Beat in egg yolks, one at a time, beating well after each addition.

Sift together flour, baking powder, and salt. Alternately mix ⅓ cup milk, then ⅓ of flour mixture into butter-egg mixture in 3 portions. Do not overmix. In another bowl, beat egg whites with clean beaters or a balloon whisk. When whites begin to foam, add remaining 1 tablespoon sugar and beat until they hold soft peaks. Scrape ½ the whites into batter and mix gently until blended. Fold in remaining whites carefully, until just blended.

Melt remaining ½ stick butter in a large sauté pan over medium-high heat until hot. Heat until butter begins to turn brown. Remove pan from heat, add vinegar and brown sugar, and mix well. (A sauce whisk is a good tool to use here.) Return to heat to melt sugar, if necessary. Pour a little of the brown sugar sauce in the bottom of the ramekins or baking pan. Cut each pineapple ring into pieces, maintaining the shape of the ring (see Chef's Notes). Add 1 pineapple ring to each ramekin or line the bottom of the large pan.

Drizzle pineapple with remaining brown sugar sauce and sprinkle with nuts. Divide batter among ramekins or pour into baking pan. Level and place in preheated oven. Bake until a tester inserted into the middle comes out clean, about 30 minutes for individual cakes or about 50 minutes for the large cake. Remove from oven and let cool about 10 minutes in the pan. Run a knife around the edges to loosen the cake(s) and invert onto deep dessert plates or a deep platter (otherwise, the sweet syrup may overflow the plate!).

Serves 6.

CHEF'S NOTES: *It does not matter whether you use light or dark brown sugar. It depends on your preference and what you might have in your cabinet. Some people do not care for the stronger molasses flavor of dark brown sugar; others are disappointed in the flavor of light. It makes no difference to the cake. I suggest cutting the pineapple ring into pieces because whole rounds can be hard to cut when baked. The ring shape is decorative but not essential.*

ROASTED PEARS WITH CINNAMON-SPICED WHIPPED CREAM

This is a delicious dessert to make when pears are in season. Cooking the fruit in mango vinegar gives an exotic, unexpected flavor, which is at once intense and balanced. The vinegar keeps the syrup from becoming cloyingly sweet. Serve the pears simply with their whipped cream garnish or with frozen yogurt or ice cream. Strew the top with chopped nuts or crushed cookies such as biscotti.

3	tablespoons dark brown sugar
4	tablespoons granulated sugar
6	tablespoons muscat grape juice (about 1 cup grapes, crushed in blender, strained, then juice measured)
¾	cup mango vinegar (page 17)
1¼	teaspoons ground cinnamon
¼	teaspoon freshly ground pepper
4	ripe pears, peeled, halved, and cored (leave stems on for presentation, if desired)
3	tablespoons unsalted butter
½	cup heavy cream
1–2	tablespoons toasted, roughly chopped pistachios (see Glossary)

Bring brown sugar, 2 tablespoons granulated sugar, and grape juice to a boil in a small, nonreactive saucepan. Stir to make sure sugar has dissolved. Remove from heat, add vinegar, 1 teaspoon cinnamon, and pepper. Stir again.

Preheat oven to 450°F. Place pears in a nonreactive bowl or shallow dish and pour vinegar mixture over them. Toss to coat well and let marinate a few minutes, while oven preheats. Drain pears and reserve syrup.

In a nonreactive, ovenproof sauté pan large enough to hold the pears in one layer, heat butter over medium-high heat until butter begins to brown. Add pears and sear on each side until lightly browned, 1 to 2 minutes per side. Add reserved syrup and toss to coat fruit well. Place in preheated oven and bake until tender, about 15 minutes, basting with pan juices once or twice.

Remove from oven and let cool about 10 minutes in cooking liquid. Remove pears to a plate and bring cooking liquid to a boil over medium-high heat. Cook until reduced by about ¼ to a light syrup consistency. (Recipe may be prepared ahead to here.)

When ready to serve, whip cream in a bowl. When cream begins to foam, add remaining 2 tablespoons granulated sugar by small spoonfuls. When cream forms soft peaks, fold in remaining ¼ teaspoon cinnamon.

Divide pears and cooking syrup among 4 plates and top with cinnamon-spiced whipped cream and chopped nuts.

Serves 4.

Savory Vinegar

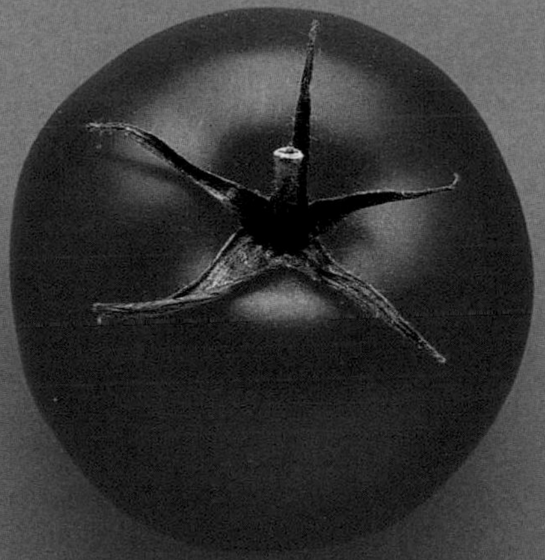

Making savory vinegars at TraVigne grew naturally out of the same inspiration that created fruit vinegars. We are constantly looking for ways to bring new flavors into each dish on our restaurant menus. Each dish must be complete in itself, incorporating many tastes and textures. For example, I might put a tuft of pea sprout tendrils on top of a rich piece of fish which is itself on a bed of lentils. But how should the pea tendrils be dressed? I want to accent the fish, not weigh it down with another oil-based vinaigrette. Savory vinegars provide a great solution because they are intensely flavored and bright tasting. They allow me—and you—to add a zap of flavor and close to no fat.

Savory vinegars have turned out to be as flexible in cooking as fruit vinegars. They make wonderful sandwich spreads on their own or sauces for vegetables, pasta, meat, and poultry. They can be turned into vinaigrettes usually with the addition of only one equal part of oil instead of the usual ratio of one part vinegar to three parts oil.

Like fruit vinegars, savory vinegars are vinegar-flavored purées as opposed to anyone's mental image of vinegar. The vinegar preserves the vegetables so these savory vinegars will keep, refrigerated, for about a week and reward the effort of making them. For long storage, I would recommend putting them in sterilized bottles and then boiling in a hot water bath for 30 minutes to preserve them. (See next column.)

Savory vinegars allow a cook to use the garden's bumper crop of produce or to take advantage of supermarket specials. Red peppers, for instance, can be quite inexpensive in season and then go up to three, four, and even five dollars a pound. But if purchased, roasted, peeled, puréed, then turned into a vinegar, the peppers will be available when you need them.

Just about anything that can be roasted and preserved will work as a savory vinegar. For example, roasted red peppers are wonderful as a vinegar—try experimenting with combinations of hot and sweet peppers. Or try a grilled eggplant vinegar, perhaps combining it with roasted garlic or caramelized onion. Shallots and green onion vinegar would also be delicious.

I have given you recipes for three savory vinegars: tomato, roasted garlic, and caramelized onion. You can even vary the flavor of these by adding fresh herbs or using an herb-flavored vinegar instead of plain champagne vinegar.

Savory vinegars are terrific to have on hand to add an extra punch of flavor to many dishes. They can be used as sauces by themselves and make delicious and unusual vinaigrettes when mixed with equal parts oil. Use Spanish or French extra-virgin olive oil to mix with savory vinegar, not Italian or Californian. These latter oils often have too assertive a flavor to complement savory vinegar. You can also use a good quality, non-virgin olive oil that is clean and neutral tasting.

If you make larger batches of savory vinegars to give as gifts or to have on hand, you should preserve them in a boiling-water bath. Sterilize bottles, jars, and tops or stoppers by running them through the dishwasher or in a hot water bath. For the latter, place the open containers on a rack or on a folded towel in a large kettle. Add water to cover, bring to a boil, and boil 15 minutes. Keep in the hot water until ready to fill. Follow manufacturer's instructions for lids and stoppers, if available. If not, put in a saucepan of water, bring to a boil, lower heat, and keep hot until needed. If you have purchased new corks, these are usually sterilized by the manufacturer.

To process the filled, closed containers, put a rack or folded tea towel on the bottom of the preserving kettle. Half fill the kettle with hot or boiling water. Place the jars or bottles in the kettle so they do not touch each other. Add more boiling water to cover the containers by about two inches. Bring the water to a rolling boil, cover, and process 30 minutes. Lift the containers out with tongs and let cool on a folded towel or wooden board in a draft-free spot.

TOMATO VINEGAR

Use this vinegar as a sauce for fried fish, pork, turkey breast, and for pasta salads. It is also good as a dip for grilled oysters and mussels. When making a vinaigrette, combine tomato vinegar with oil in equal parts. In the summer, when tomatoes are really ripe, omit the sun-dried tomatoes altogether. Cut the vine-ripened tomatoes into chunks and cook them down but do not purée them, so the vinegar will have texture.

1	tablespoon olive oil
1	tablespoon minced garlic
1	cup peeled, seeded, and chopped vine-ripe tomatoes or good quality canned plum (Roma) tomatoes
¼–1	cup water
4	ounces sun-dried tomatoes in oil (½ an 8-ounce jar), well drained, or 3 ounces dried tomatoes, rehydrated in water
	Salt and freshly ground pepper
½	cup champagne vinegar (6 percent acidity) or herbal vinegar (page 82) flavored with basil
2	tablespoons finely chopped fresh basil (optional)

Heat oil in a small sauté pan over medium-high heat until almost smoking. Add garlic and sauté, moving pan off and on heat to regulate temperature, until light brown. Add tomatoes, ¼ cup water, and bring to a boil. Reduce heat to medium and simmer until thick. Add sun-dried tomatoes and cook until they soften, about 3 minutes. Season with salt and pepper.

Purée tomato mixture in a blender. Add vinegar and thin with remaining water, if necessary. Pulse in basil if using. Adjust seasoning with salt, pepper, and vinegar. Pour into a bowl or pitcher, then transfer to a clean, wide-mouthed bottle or jar and cover with a non-metallic lid. Keeps, refrigerated, about 1 week.

Makes about 2 cups.

CARAMELIZED ONION VINEGAR

Caramelized onion makes an amazingly rich and deep vinegar which has become my new favorite. It is a great spread for sandwiches such as pot roast with cheese. It is also delicious with pork chops and liver.

3	tablespoons extra-virgin olive oil
3	large onions, finely chopped
	Salt and freshly ground pepper
1	cup champagne vinegar (6 percent acidity)
	About ¼ cup water
½	tablespoon finely chopped fresh thyme (optional)

Heat olive oil in a large, heavy sauté pan over medium-high heat until almost smoking. Add onions, reduce heat to medium or medium-low, and sauté onions until well caramelized and dark brown, about 45 minutes or as long as you have the patience! Be careful to stir well and to regulate temperature so onions do not burn but caramelize slowly. Season with salt and pepper. You should have about 1 cup caramelized onions.

Transfer onions to a blender and purée with vinegar. Thin with water if necessary so that mixture is the texture of a very thick, smooth sauce. Pulse in thyme, if using. Adjust flavor with salt, pepper, and vinegar. Scrape into a clean, wide-mouthed bottle or jar and cover with a nonmetallic lid. Keeps, refrigerated, about a week.

Makes about 1¾ cups.

ROASTED GARLIC VINEGAR

Roasted garlic vinegar, like the other savory vinegars, will never win the ketchup race! It is quite thick, not as thick as mayonnaise, but very like a mayonnaise thinned enough to make it barely pourable. Mix this vinegar with equal parts olive oil for a great dressing for egg and tuna salads.

8	large, whole heads garlic
1	cup extra-virgin olive oil
	Salt and freshly ground pepper
1	cup champagne vinegar (6 percent acidity)
	About ¼ cup water

Preheat oven to 375°F. Cut off the top ½ inch of each garlic head. Peel off outer layers of papery skin and place heads in a shallow baking dish just large enough to hold them in one layer. Pour oil over them and season with salt and pepper. Cover, place in oven, and cook until cloves are soft and begin to push out of their skins, about 1 hour. Uncover and bake until golden brown, about 15 minutes. Let cool, then squeeze the softened cloves from their skins into a bowl and mash. You should have about 1 cup. Strain the cooking oil into a clean bottle and refrigerate to use for all sorts of sautés, for drizzling over meat and poultry, or for salad dressings.

Put the roasted garlic paste into a blender and add vinegar. Blend until smooth and adjust seasoning with salt, pepper, and vinegar. Add water to thin if necessary. Scrape into a clean, wide-mouthed bottle or jar and cover with a nonmetallic lid. Keeps, refrigerated, about a week.

Makes about 1¾ cups.

CARPACCIO OF BEETS WITH GOAT CHEESE

I am convinced that Americans' seeming lack of enthusiasm for beets is because they have never tasted a properly cooked one. Who could resist the rich, sweet taste and yielding texture of beets roasted in their jackets? As an added bonus, cooking them in their skins maintains their high nutritive value. I love the flavor of beets with raspberry and mango vinegar. When beets are in season, make a spectacular presentation by combining red, golden, and Ciogga (variegated) beets.

4	medium-sized beets
3	tablespoons extra-virgin olive oil
	Salt and freshly ground pepper
2	tablespoons caramelized onion vinegar (page 36)
2	cups (about) mixed baby salad greens
2	tablespoons fresh goat cheese
1½	tablespoons raspberry vinegar (page 17) or mango vinegar (page 17)

Preheat oven to 400°F. Brush beets with 1 tablespoon olive oil, season with salt and pepper, and place in a baking dish. Bake until beets are very tender, 1 to 2 hours. Remove and let rest until cool enough to handle. Peel and slice very, very thin on a mandoline. Arrange slices, slightly overlapping in a petal pattern, on each of 4 salad plates. Drizzle with 1 tablespoon olive oil and 1 tablespoon onion vinegar. Sprinkle lightly with salt and pepper.

Toss salad greens in a bowl with remaining 1 tablespoon olive oil, remaining 1 tablespoon onion vinegar, and salt and pepper. Arrange a small pile in the middle of the beets. Crumble goat cheese over each salad and drizzle with fruit vinegar.

Serves 4.

GRILLED MOZZARELLA WITH TOMATO VINEGAR

This salad had an almost cultlike following at TraVigne for years. The salad eventually came off the menu only to make room for new dishes. One of my partner's wives still insists I make it for her every time she comes in. It is a great warm salad for early fall though it was so popular we served it year round. Serve it for lunch or supper or as an appetizer at dinner.

4	very large romaine leaves
8	ounces fresh mozzarella cheese, cut into 4 equal pieces
	Salt and freshly ground pepper
1½	ounces prosciutto, diced
1	tablespoon extra-virgin olive oil
6	tablespoons (about) tomato vinegar (page 36)
2	tablespoons Spanish or French extra-virgin olive oil
1	large bunch arugula, watercress, or other crisp, spicy green
2	tablespoons freshly grated Parmesan cheese

Bring a pot of salted water to a boil. Blanch romaine until color is bright green and central rib is just tender enough to bend, about 30 seconds. Remove and immediately plunge romaine into ice water to stop the cooking. Drain and pat dry.

Prepare grill or preheat broiler. Lay romaine leaves out on a counter, rib side down. Cut out the widest part of the central rib by making a triangular cut at the base of each leaf. Place a square of cheese in the middle of each leaf. Season with salt and pepper. Sprinkle each with about 1 tablespoon prosciutto. Make a neat package by folding the leaves around the cheese like an envelope, ending seam side down. Brush each with olive oil.

Spread about 1 tablespoon tomato vinegar in the center of each of 4 salad plates. In a bowl, whisk together remaining 2 tablespoons vinegar and Spanish or French olive oil. Add arugula and toss to lightly dress. Taste and add more vinegar, salt, and pepper, if necessary. Arrange equal portions in a wreath on each plate. Sprinkle greens with Parmesan.

Grill cheese packages over medium heat or put in a preheated broiler about 4 inches from the heat. Cook 2 to 3 minutes and turn over. Cook another 1 to 2 minutes or just until cheese begins to weep. Packages should be soft to the touch and lightly brown. Do not let cheese get too hot or it will toughen as it cools. Set grilled mozzarella in center of plates and serve immediately.

Serves 4.

PORK SHORT STACK

I created this as a two-ingredient supper dish. While it looks elegant, it is simply sautéed pork with a pan sauce. Serve it with applesauce flavored with fruit vinegar. To vary the flavor, make the sauce one week with roasted garlic vinegar and the next with caramelized onion or tomato vinegar.

2	cups chicken stock (page 20) or low-salt, canned chicken broth
8	slices pork loin (2 to 3 ounces each and about 2 inches thick)
	Salt and freshly ground pepper
	Flour for dredging
2	tablespoons extra-virgin olive oil
1	tablespoon finely chopped fresh sage
3	tablespoons roasted garlic vinegar (page 37)
1	small bunch, pencil-thin asparagus spears (about ½ pound), cut to about 5 inches long
1	tablespoon finely chopped fresh flat-leaf parsley

Bring stock to a boil in a saucepan and boil until reduced by about ½. Reserve.

Butterfly each piece of meat by making a horizontal cut not quite all the way through and open like the pages of a book. Pound each slice lightly between sheets of waxed paper into thin scaloppine, about ¼ inch thick. Season with salt and pepper and dredge with flour. Heat oil in a large sauté pan over medium-high heat until almost smoking. Add pork (do not crowd the pan). Immediately reduce heat to medium and cook without turning until blood droplets rise to the top surface, about 30 seconds. Turn and cook the second side, about another 30 seconds. Pork should be done at this point. If not, continue to cook until done. Remove to a plate and keep warm.

Add sage to the hot sauté pan, stir, and add reduced stock and vinegar. Stir up any browned bits that cling to the bottom and sides of the pan. Bring to a boil and boil until reduced to a saucelike consistency, about ¾ cup.

Meanwhile, bring a large pot of salted water to a boil. Add asparagus and cook until bright green and tender, about 2 minutes. Drain.

To serve, arrange one piece of pork on each of 4 heated dinner plates. Divide half the asparagus among the plates, arranging it on top of the pork. Top with another slice of pork and the remaining asparagus. Spoon sauce over each and garnish with parsley.

Serves 4.

ROASTED GARLIC PENNE
WITH ASPARAGUS
AND SHIITAKE MUSHROOMS

This is a hearty-tasting pasta without being at all heavy. It has a good rich taste from the roasted garlic and mushrooms, but the vinegar flavor keeps the palate fresh. My basic rule is to cut vegetables the same size as the pasta shape—when that makes sense, as it does here with fusilli. I also like pasta dishes that are composed of 30 to 40 percent other ingredients. You can substitute green beans for asparagus to take advantage of the changing seasons.

¾ pound asparagus, peeled if jumbo sized,
   cut into 1½-inch pieces
1 pound dried penne pasta
3 tablespoons extra-virgin olive oil
1 tablespoon butter
4 cups thinly sliced fresh shiitake mushrooms
1 tablespoon finely chopped fresh thyme
   Salt and freshly ground pepper
2 cups chicken stock (page 20) or low-salt,
   canned chicken broth
3 tablespoons roasted garlic vinegar
   (page 37) or more to taste
3 tablespoons finely chopped fresh
   flat-leaf parsley
½ cup freshly grated Parmesan cheese
2 tablespoons toasted pine nuts (see Glossary)

Bring a large pot of salted water to a boil. Add asparagus and cook just until bright green and slightly tender, about 2 minutes. Dip out with a strainer and spread on a baking sheet to cool. Return water to a boil, add pasta, and stir. Cook pasta until al dente and drain.

Meanwhile, heat olive oil in a large, deep sauté pan over medium-high heat until almost smoking. Add butter, then mushrooms in a single layer. Do not move mushrooms until browned on one side, about 1 minute. Then sauté until brown, about 5 minutes. Add thyme, then asparagus, and sauté another 15 to 20 seconds. Season with salt and pepper and add stock. Bring to a boil and cook until reduced by about ⅓. Stir in vinegar.

Add drained pasta to the sauté pan and toss well. (If you do not have a pan large enough to hold all the pasta, return cooked pasta to pasta pot and pour sauce over it.) Taste for seasoning and adjust with more vinegar, if desired, and salt and pepper. Add parsley and ¾ of the cheese. Toss well. Serve sprinkled with pine nuts and remaining cheese.

Serves 4 to 6.

Balsamic Vinegar

My first taste of traditional balsamic vinegar was on a wild strawberry picking expedition just outside the Italian town of Modena. We put a drop of the almost black, exotic, fragrant, sweet-tart vinegar on the tip of each berry as we picked and ate. That is about as perfect as food can get.

I was visiting Modena, the birthplace and home of *aceto balsamico tradizionale*, to study how this precious vinegar is made. The balsamic vinegar with which most of us are familiar, selling in specialty stores and supermarkets from $3.99 up, is not traditional balsamic vinegar. It is instead, a decent wine vinegar meant to mimic the flavor of the traditional balsamic. These commercial vinegars are made in Modena and throughout Italy and are called *aceto balsamico di Modena* (the word *tradizionale* is missing). They are flavored with herbs and caramel and aged in wood. Longer aging usually translates to better taste.

The traditional vinegar may only be made in Modena and neighboring Reggio, both in the heart of Emilia-Romagna, itself the heart of Italy. Italian law protects the quality of this traditional and ancient vinegar. While the term *aceto balsamico* and a written recipe for the vinegar date only from the eighteenth century, *aceto* existed long before—the first recorded history of *aceto* notes that in 1046 Bonifacio di Canossa, the Marquis of Bologna and Modena, gave a barrel of it to Henry III, the Holy Roman Emperor, as a coronation gift.

The regulations direct all facets of vinegar making from the type of grape used for the base wine, and its aging in graduated sets of wood barrels called *batterias*, to its bottling. To be sold as *aceto balsamico tradizionale*, the vinegar must be at least twelve years old and is often much older. It also must pass a taste test by the Consortium of Producers of Traditional Balsamic Vinegar and be bottled only in 100 cc (3.3 ounce) bottles. These little bottles of vinegar are fabulously expensive, but one sniff of an *aceto balsamico tradizionale* gives explanation enough.

The expense of this dense, dark brown, syrupy vinegar with its seductive, characteristic scents of herbs and woods depends on two factors: the length of time it takes to make—twelve years minimum—and the very large amount of source material needed to produce even a small amount of vinegar. The traditional vinegar differs from all other vinegar in that the grape juice is concentrated before the alcoholic and the vinegar fermentations begin.

Every *aceto balsamico* producer has his or her cherished variations on the methods prescribed by the government. Traditionally, it is women who are the vinegar makers, but this is not required by law! A *batteria* of *aceto balsamico* was often part of a young woman's dowry.

Several grape types are used, but the most common is Trebbiano. The grapes are picked for vinegar making when very ripe and full of sugar. They are crushed to release their juice and then the juice is separated from the pulp, seeds, and skins. The juice is then poured into large copper cauldrons suspended over wood fires. The juice is brought to a boil and boiled until reduced by 30 percent to 50 percent of its original volume. This very sweet juice (also called "must") is then transferred to the first barrel of the *batteria* in the late fall and inoculated with yeast for the alcoholic fermentation and with active vinegar from another barrel in the *batteria*. The *batteria* is usually housed in an attic where the temperature fluctuations, from very cold in the winter to quite hot in the summer, play an important part in the creation of *aceto balsamico tradizionale*.

During the following winter, the cold inhibits both fermentations and allows the solids to precipitate out of suspension and the liquid to clear. Once the warmth of spring reaches the barrels, the cooked juice begins a slow alcoholic fermentation. The vinegar fermentation, encouraged by the heat of spring and summer, goes on simultaneously: as the alcohol forms, it is changed into acetic acid. By the end of summer, both fermentations will be complete and the ensuing cold allows the vinegar to clarify again.

In the spring, this new vinegar will begin its passage through the *batteria*. Over the years in the attic, the vinegar moves from one barrel to the next, each one smaller than the one before. The largest is probably only 50 liters and the smallest is about 10 liters. By law, there must be at least three sizes of barrels in each *batteria*. The barrels of a *batteria* may all be made out of the same type of wood or from several types. The choice of wood is limited to oak, chestnut, ash, mulberry, juniper, locust, and cherry. Each of the various woods adds a new flavor to the vinegar while evaporation claims about 10 percent of the volume each year.

Once a year, from the smallest, oldest barrel, about one liter of vinegar is drawn off for sale or home use. At the end of the required twelve-year aging period, hundreds of liters of fresh grape juice have been reduced to a few liters of intensely flavored, aromatic vinegar that tastes harmoniously sweet and tart at once.

It is only fairly recently that *aceto balsamico tradizionale* has become available for sale in the United States. Usually, it was reserved to be given as gifts or used by the thimbleful by the family and then only on special occasions.

Many positive health claims are made for this powerful and unique vinegar. The term *balsamico*, as used with *aceto*, implies having restorative powers. It has been considered a cure-all and health tonic for centuries and even to have particular benefits for men. When I questioned a number of the finer producers in Modena about this, however, their answers were always the same: "It might be so, but we Modenese have no need of such a thing, and so we would not know!"

If you should be so lucky as to acquire a bottle of the real *aceto balsamico tradizionale*, you may be tempted to just open and sniff it occasionally. It is heady stuff! But do use it: sprinkle it—drop by drop, as the Modenese do—on ripe strawberries where the aromatic properties of the vinegar appear to intensify the "strawberryness," or on a freshly grilled, rare steak. It is also delicious drizzled on freshly grilled wild mushrooms, on slivers of Parmesan cheese (an example of the marriage of two compatible local products, Parmesan also being made in that region), on grilled or roasted chicken and game birds. If you use traditional balsamic vinegar for a salad dressing, use just a few drops of the traditional vinegar to "correct" the flavor of the wine vinegar. You will be amazed at its effect!

You can afford to be much more generous with commercial balsamic vinegar. There are many brands available at many price points. Choose a vinegar that smells pleasantly of a rich blend of herbal and woodsy scents and has a smooth, rich taste both sweet and tart.

Balsamic syrup is a terrific basic ingredient to keep on hand. Since there is really nothing to do but let the pot boil and the vinegar reduce, it is easy to make while working on other projects in the kitchen. Use inexpensive, commercial balsamic vinegar. Be sure to taste the vinegar to make sure you like its flavor, as reducing it to a syrup will magnify its flavors. Use the syrup as a substitute for the very expensive traditional balsamico; spread a teaspoon of it over a freshly cooked steak with ½ teaspoon coarse salt; sprinkle it on raw or cooked fruit; add a spoonful to sauces. I especially like to use the syrup for "broken" vinaigrettes: I sprinkle extra-virgin olive oil on a dish, then sprinkle on a little syrup. A pattern of green and dark brown forms and makes a dish such as fresh mozzarella sparkle. A regular vinaigrette might discolor the very white, fresh cheese.

2   cups commercial balsamic vinegar
     (6 percent acidity)

Put the vinegar in a nonreactive saucepan and bring to a boil over medium-high heat. Boil until reduced to a very thick syrup. When it is reduced enough, the bubbles forming on top will be very small. Do not get too close to the pan; the vinegar fumes may make it hard to breathe. Pour the syrup into a small glass jar or bottle, and seal with a nonmetallic cap.

Makes about 6 tablespoons.

BALSAMIC ROASTED ONIONS

I was inspired to create a recipe for these onions by an alfresco meal in Milan. I had been to Peck's and bought a picnic—crusty bread, olives, cippolini onions, and more—then sat, eating in the sun, on the steps of the Duomo. The onions were so spectacular that I took pictures of them and when I got back home, I worked out how to make them. Serve these onions with braised short ribs of beef (page 75), chicken, carpaccio of beets with goat cheese (page 37), or as part of an antipasto. Choose the fresh herb for the recipe to complement whatever dish you plan to serve with the onions. Make lots of them; once you taste how delicious they are, you will find many opportunities to serve them. They will keep, refrigerated, for about a week. You can make the recipe with shallots as well. Boil just until tender; shallots will not take as long as the onions.

	Salt and freshly ground pepper
1	pound boiling onions (about 1 inch in diameter), peeled and left whole
2	tablespoons extra-virgin olive oil
1	tablespoon finely chopped fresh thyme, fresh rosemary, or other herb
½	cup balsamic vinegar

Bring a large pot of heavily salted water to a boil. Add onions and boil until tender but still firm, about 12 minutes. When you insert a knife in an onion, it should meet just a little resistance in the center. Drain onions and spread on a baking sheet to cool.

Preheat oven to 450°F. Heat olive oil in a non-reactive oven-going sauté pan (just large enough to hold onions in one layer) over medium-high heat until hot. Add onions, season with pepper, and sauté until they are browned and caramelized all over, about 5 minutes. Add thyme and sauté another few seconds. Standing back to avoid being spattered, add vinegar, bring to a boil, and roll onions around in vinegar to coat well. Put in pre-heated oven until very tender and vinegar has reduced to a glaze, about 10 minutes. Remove onions at least once during cooking and toss well before returning pan to oven. Let onions cool in pan and toss occasionally so vinegar adheres to onions as they cool. Serve at room temperature or while still warm.

Serves 6.

ROASTED FALL FRUIT SALAD WITH PARMESAN GELATO

Serve this fruit "salad" as a cheese course and it will take care of dessert as well. The roasted fruit makes a great backdrop for the intense flavor of traditional balsamic vinegar. Parmesan gelato sounds exotic but is very simple to make and can be done ahead. The cool temperature and surprising flavor of the gelato make a stunning contrast with the warmth and sweetness of the fruit and croutons. Chose crisp, ripe, flavorful fruits. If pressed for time, you can serve the fruit without cooking. Just sprinkle the vinegar over it. When persimmons are out of season, use more apples and pears. The pomegranate adds color and texture but is not mandatory.

PARMESAN GELATO
- ⅔ cup heavy cream
- ¾ cup freshly grated Parmesan cheese

FALL FRUIT SALAD
- 3–4 tablespoons unsalted butter
- ½ baguette, cut diagonally into thin slices
  Salt and freshly ground pepper
- 1 bay leaf
- 1 large crisp apple (such as pippin or Granny Smith), peeled, cored, and cut into 1-inch chunks
- 2 large ripe pears (such as d'Anjou), peeled, cored, and cut into 1-inch chunks
- 2 Japanese persimmons, cut into 1-inch chunks
- 1 small pomegranate (optional), peeled and seeds reserved
- 1 tablespoon traditional balsamic vinegar or balsamic syrup (page 48)

TO MAKE GELATO: Put the cream and Parmesan in the top of a double boiler and place over simmering water. Heat until cheese has thoroughly melted into the milk, about 3 minutes. Whisk occasionally. Strain through a medium-mesh sieve into a small bowl. Do not press on the cheese solids. Discard solids. Cover cheese-cream mixture and refrigerate overnight. The cheese gelato should harden to a spreadable consistency. If it does not, move it to the freezer until firm. Return gelato to refrigerator for a short while before serving to soften slightly.

FOR FALL FRUIT SALAD: Preheat oven to 350°F. Melt 1 to 2 tablespoons butter in a large, ovenproof skillet over medium heat until hot. Add bread and toss to coat well. Season with salt and pepper. Place pan in oven and toast bread until crispy and brown all over, about 15 minutes. Turn pieces occasionally to make sure they brown evenly. Remove, drain on paper towels, and reserve. Croutons may be prepared several hours ahead of time.

Preheat broiler. Heat remaining 2 tablespoons butter in another ovenproof skillet over medium-high heat until hot. Add bay leaf, then apple, pears, persimmons, and salt and pepper to taste. Toss well so all fruit is covered with butter and increase heat to medium high just until pan is hot again. Immediately put pan under preheated broiler and broil until fruit begins to caramelize, about 5 minutes. Check fruit frequently and toss well each time. Fruit should be tender yet a little firm in the center. Pour fruit onto a baking sheet to cool to room temperature. Discard bay leaf.

Arrange a mixture of cooked fruit on each of 4 plates. Sprinkle with pomegranate seeds (if using) and balsamic vinegar or syrup. Add 1 or 2 croutons to each and a scoop of Parmesan gelato.

Serves 4.

ROASTED POLENTA WITH MUSHROOMS AND BALSAMIC SAUCE

This dish quickly became a signature dish for TraVigne. It is also the single most often requested recipe by our customers! It can be turned into a festive occasion by inviting a few friends over and asking each to bring a part of the recipe. The butter that finishes the sauce may be omitted but it marries the richness of the dish to the sharpness of the vinegar.

	Polenta (page 54)
½	cup (about) freshly grated Parmesan cheese
	Balsamic sauce (recipe follows), without final butter
½	stick (4 tablespoons) unsalted butter
	Salt and freshly ground pepper
2	tablespoons extra-virgin olive oil
2	cups sliced domestic or shiitake mushrooms
1	tablespoon finely chopped garlic
1	teaspoon chopped fresh thyme
1	tablespoon finely chopped fresh flat-leaf parsley

Preheat oven to 500°F. Cut prepared polenta into squares or triangles and sprinkle with Parmesan. Place on a lightly buttered baking sheet and roast in the oven until cheese is lightly browned, 6 to 8 minutes. Remove and keep warm.

Heat the balsamic sauce in a nonreactive saucepan over medium heat until hot and whisk in butter by the tablespoonful. Season to taste with pepper. Keep warm.

Heat olive oil in a sauté pan over medium-high heat until almost smoking. Add mushrooms and do not move them until lightly brown on one side, about 1 minute. Add garlic and sauté until mushrooms are brown, about 5 minutes. (It is very important that the mushrooms are not crowded; otherwise they will boil in their own juices rather than brown.) Add thyme and parsley and adjust seasoning with salt and pepper.

To serve, divide sauce among 6 hot plates. Top with roasted polenta then mushrooms. Serve immediately.

Serves 6.

BALSAMIC SAUCE

Balsamic sauce is a very intense, concentrated sauce that makes simple polenta a dish fit for royalty. It needs strong flavors to match its power, for instance, steak or venison. While balsamic sauce does take time to make, it is not at all complicated and can be refrigerated or frozen. Make a batch and keep it on hand for a really cold night when a bowl of polenta with balsamic sauce will be sure to make you feel warm and well taken care of.

2	cups balsamic vinegar
1	shallot, chopped
8	cups roasted chicken stock (page 20) or low-salt, canned chicken broth (see Chef's Notes)
2	bay leaves
6	peppercorns
½	stick (4 tablespoons) unsalted butter (optional)
	Salt and freshly ground pepper

Bring vinegar and shallot to a boil over high heat in a large, heavy nonreactive saucepan. Boil until reduced to a syrup consistency. Add stock, bay leaves, and peppercorns. Bring to a boil again and continue to cook until reduced to about 2 cups or less. The consistency should be very thick, not quite returned to a syrup but bordering it. Let cool slightly, then strain through a fine sieve.

At this point the sauce is ready to be used in the Roasted Polenta with Mushrooms and Balsamic Sauce (earlier this page), covered and refrigerated or frozen for later use, or finished with butter for immediate use.

To use as a sauce on its own: Heat balsamic reduction over moderate heat until hot and whisk in the butter by spoonfuls. Season with salt and pepper to taste.

Makes about 2 cups.

CHEF'S NOTES: *You can use a brown chicken stock, veal, or rabbit stock, or a combination. I like to use chicken and veal. If using canned broth, do not salt any part of the recipe until final adjustment.*

POLENTA

This is the very best recipe for polenta I have ever used. The ratio of liquid and dry ingredients is three to one. It is unusual in that it calls for equal parts polenta and semolina. The semolina ensures that the cream does not separate out of the mixture. It also allows the dish to cook more quickly and gives it a smoother texture. The polenta should freeze very well if you want to double or triple the recipe. Just be sure to separate layers with wax paper. Polenta can be served as is; sprinkled with Parmesan and gratinéed; brushed with oil and grilled, toasted, or sautéed; served with tomato sauce; or just with browned butter.

1½ cups roasted chicken stock (page 20)
    or low-salt, canned chicken broth
1½ cups heavy cream
    Pinch freshly grated nutmeg
¾ teaspoon salt
    Pinch ground white pepper
½ cup polenta (see Glossary)
½ cup semolina (see Glossary)
¼ cup freshly grated fontina cheese
¼ cup freshly grated Parmesan cheese
    Butter for baking sheet

Combine stock, cream, nutmeg, salt, and pepper in a large, heavy pot. Bring liquid to a boil, then add polenta and semolina gradually while stirring with a whisk or spoon. Stir well when adding the semolina as it tends to clump.

Continue to cook over moderate heat while stirring constantly. Polenta is ready when it pulls away from the sides of the pot, about 5 minutes, and takes on a choux paste (cream puff pastry) texture.

Remove from heat and sprinkle in fontina and Parmesan. Let sit a few moments to allow for cheese to soften, then mix in. If cheese gets too hot, the texture will be grainy. Line an 8 x 8-inch baking pan with buttered waxed paper; be sure pan is not warped. Using a flat, metal spatula, spread polenta evenly in prepared pan. Spread polenta to a thickness of approximately ½ inch. Smooth with the spatula.

Cool to room temperature, then cover with waxed paper or parchment and refrigerate. Polenta should be prepared at least 4 hours in advance so it has a chance to set up. Once it has set up, cut into portion sizes such as squares or triangles. Wrap well to freeze or refrigerate for a day before use.

Serves 6.

This vegetable stew is a whimsical adaptation of an old idea—making a meal out of what is abundant and at hand. A brodetto is actually a fisherman's stew made of odds and ends of unsold fish and seafood. To me, a brodetto now has come to mean a dish that takes advantage of abundant seasonal ingredients. Put this vegetable stew over pasta or under fish. When I use it as a pasta sauce, I add basil. If it is to be served with a rich fish, I flavor the stew with savory. I particularly like it as a fall dish to serve with pheasant and then I use sage. To make a colorful dish, I like to use yellow tomatoes and roasted red peppers. Or use red tomatoes and roasted yellow peppers.

1	large bunch green or red Swiss chard
2	tablespoons extra-virgin olive oil
1	tablespoon finely chopped garlic
¼	cup balsamic vinegar
1	cup peeled, seeded, and coarsely chopped tomato (1-inch pieces)
1	red bell pepper, roasted, seeded, and cut into 1-inch pieces (see Glossary)
1	cup chicken stock (page 20) or low-salt, canned chicken broth
	Salt and freshly ground pepper
1	tablespoon finely chopped fresh herb (such as basil, savory, or sage)
2	tablespoons butter

Remove tough portions of chard stems by placing leaves flat on a cutting board and making a triangular cut in the base of the leaves. Then stack the leaves and cut them into 1-inch strips. Turn the strips 90 degrees and cut them into 1-inch pieces.

Heat olive oil in a nonreactive sauté pan over medium-high heat until almost smoking. Add garlic and sauté until light brown, about 1 minute, moving pan off and on heat as needed to regulate temperature. With pan off heat so it does not spit too ferociously, add vinegar, tomatoes, and roasted pepper. Return pan to heat and bring to a boil. Add stock, return to a boil, and boil until reduced by about half, or until slightly thickened. Season with salt and pepper to taste, add herb, stir well, then add chard. Cook just until chard has wilted into the sauce. Stir in butter and serve.

Serves 3 to 4.

CHEF'S NOTES: *If the chard is overgrown and has very large leaves, blanch it first in boiling salted water for 20 seconds. Immediately plunge the greens in ice water to stop the cooking, squeeze out the water, and roughly chop the leaves. The quick blanching removes some of the bitterness of late-season, overgrown chard.*

PUMPKIN RAVIOLI WITH PAILLARD OF TURKEY BREAST AND CRANBERRY BROWN BUTTER

This dish was originally created as a Thanksgiving dinner for two as it combines the favorite flavors of the season—pumpkin, turkey, and cranberries—but in a surprising way and without having to roast a whole turkey: The paillard is simply a piece of uncooked turkey breast pounded to an even, ¼-inch thickness. The separate elements of the dish can be enjoyed on their own as well: The turkey alone with the sauce, or the raviolis with the sauce and without the turkey, or the raviolis on their own served with warmed butter and sage.

4	portions boneless turkey breast (4 ounces each)
2	tablespoons extra-virgin olive oil Salt and freshly ground pepper
½	stick (4 tablespoons) unsalted butter
8	pumpkin raviolis (recipe follows)
4	shallots, minced
¾	cup fresh cranberries
2	tablespoons dark molasses
2	teaspoons minced fresh sage or 1 teaspoon dried sage
¼	cup balsamic vinegar
½	cup chicken stock (page 20) or low-salt, canned chicken broth

Bring 4 quarts lightly salted water to a boil in a large pot.

To form the turkey paillards, place turkey portions between sheets of plastic wrap. Pound to an even ¼-inch thickness.

Heat olive oil in a large sauté pan over medium-high heat. Season turkey paillards on both sides with salt and pepper. When oil is very hot, add turkey paillards. Do not crowd the pan. Let brown, about 1 minute, then turn to cook the second side, another 15 seconds. Turkey paillards cook very quickly and will dry out if overcooked. When done, remove to a baking sheet or platter and keep warm. Do not wash sauté pan!

To make the sauce, add butter to sauté pan and place over medium-high heat. At the same time, drop raviolis into the boiling water. When butter turns light brown, add shallots. Stir 10 seconds and add cranberries, molasses, sage, balsamic vinegar, and stock. Simmer until cranberries are soft, about 2 minutes. Season to taste with salt and pepper.

Test raviolis for doneness in about 3 minutes: Pinch edges of dough; it should be tender. Drain. Arrange 2 raviolis per person on hot plates and place a piece of turkey on top. Spoon sauce over them.

Serves 4.

CHEF'S NOTES: *The sauce must be put together very quickly, so have all the ingredients premeasured and ready at the side of the stove.*

This filling, with its spiced, savory flavor, can be used to stuff tortellini to serve in a rich, roast chicken broth. Or mix it with mashed sweet or white potatoes to make a gratin topped with buttery bread crumbs seasoned with nutmeg, cinnamon, and telemé cheese. The raviolis can be made ahead and frozen.

1	small white or pie pumpkin (about 2½ pounds) or Hubbard squash
2	tablespoons dark molasses
2	tablespoons unsalted butter
2	teaspoons balsamic vinegar
¼	cup mascarpone cheese
2	tablespoons freshly grated Parmesan cheese
¼	teaspoon ground cinnamon
¼	teaspoon freshly grated nutmeg
	Salt and freshly ground pepper
	Ravioli dough (recipe follows) or ¾ pound sheet pasta purchased from local Italian delicatessen
	Flour for dusting board

Preheat oven to 375°F. Cut pumpkin in half and scrape out seeds. Spread 1 tablespoon molasses in the cavity. Season with salt and pepper. Place cut side down on a roasting pan. Cook in the oven until very soft, about 1 hour. (See Chef's Notes.) Let cool to room temperature and scoop out flesh into the work bowl of a food processor.

Purée pumpkin until smooth, then spread on a baking sheet and return to the 375°F oven to dry, about 10 minutes. The consistency will be like mashed potatoes. Scrape into a large mixing bowl.

Heat the butter in a small saucepan over medium-low heat until it begins to brown. Immediately remove from heat and add remaining 1 tablespoon molasses and all the vinegar. Add to pumpkin with mascarpone, Parmesan, cinnamon, and nutmeg. Season to taste with salt and pepper and mix well. The recipe can be made ahead to this point (makes about 2 cups filling). Cover well and refrigerate 4 hours or up to 2 days.

To fill the raviolis: Lay out a sheet of pasta dough on a lightly floured board. Cut into circles with a 3½-inch pastry cutter. Put 1 tablespoon pumpkin filling in the center of half the rounds using either a pastry bag or a small spoon. Leave a ½-inch border all around the filling. Moisten borders with water and top with remaining rounds of dough. Press all the air out and seal firmly by pressing all around with fingertips. Lay raviolis out to dry on a lightly floured board or baking sheet and lightly flour the tops. Repeat until you run out of dough and/or filling. To cook, boil in lightly salted water until tender, about 3 minutes.

Uncooked, filled raviolis may be used immediately or frozen for 2 months. Lay them out on sheet pans and place in freezer until frozen. Transfer to plastic bag.

Serves 4.

CHEF'S NOTES: *While I prefer the flavor oven roasting gives the pumpkin, you can microwave the pumpkin as well for about 30 minutes, depending on the power of your oven. You will still need to dry the purée in the oven as in the recipe.*

RAVIOLI DOUGH

This is a good dough for filled pastas because the extra egg makes the dough tender and more pliable. It can be made ahead and frozen. If you do not want to make pasta dough or do not have a pasta machine, sheets of pasta are often available for purchase at your local Italian delicatessen. Recipe may be doubled.

¾	cup semolina (see Glossary)
⅞	cup unbleached all-purpose flour plus more for dusting work surface
2	extra-large eggs
	Pinch salt
1½	teaspoons extra-virgin olive oil

Place all ingredients in work bowl of a food processor and pulse until coarsely combined. If dough is too wet, sprinkle it with more flour and pulse again. Remove the dough to a lightly floured board and form into a ball. Knead dough with the palm of your hand about 1 minute, folding the dough over itself until it comes together into an easily workable mass. Let rest 30 minutes.

Cut dough into several pieces and flatten each lightly, then pass it through the widest setting on your pasta machine. Lightly flour dough, fold it in thirds and run it through the widest setting again. Repeat 3 more times. Pass dough through successively narrower settings until you can just barely see your fingers through the dough. Be sure there is a light dusting of flour on the dough at all times.

Dough may be used immediately or refrigerated up to 3 days or frozen for 2 months. Let come to room temperature before rolling.

Makes about ¾ pound dough; enough for 4 servings.

TRADITIONAL BISTECCA ALLA FIORENTINO

My mother used to make a steak very much like this. She cooked it on the flat top of the wood stove, then sprinkled the meat with vinegar and oregano she had dried herself. She was of the opinion that herbs should dry fast to maintain flavor. She harvested bouquets from the garden and hung them from the ceiling in the closet with the hot water heater. She served a chopped green salad in a wooden bowl, and I would suggest serving the Balsamic Roasted Onions (page 49) as well. This dish is a great example of simple cooking techniques showing off superb ingredients. When I make this at home, friends gnaw the bones clean before my golden retriever, Sage, gets them.

1	T-bone steak (about 2 pounds and 1½ to 2 inches thick)
	Salt and freshly ground pepper
1	tablespoon extra-virgin olive oil or roasted garlic oil (see Glossary)
2	teaspoons traditional balsamic vinegar or balsamic syrup (page 48)
1	teaspoon dried oregano
	Coarse salt

Preheat grill or a griddle or a cast iron frying pan over medium-high heat. Sprinkle steak with salt and pepper on both sides. Sear steak quickly on both sides, then cook just until blood rare, about 5 minutes per side. Remove to a cutting board and sprinkle with oil and vinegar. Crumble oregano over the meat. Let rest 5 minutes, then carve diagonally across the grain into thin slices. Sprinkle with coarse salt and serve with the meat juices from the cutting board.

Serves 4.

CHEF'S NOTES: *It is well worth investing in a cast iron liner for your grill. Cooking on the chrome-plated grill can be frustrating since food seems to stick no matter what. The cast iron insert preheats well, searing food immediately. Also, food does not seem to stick as much. Williams-Sonoma sells the insert for outdoor Weber kettles and makes one for your stove as well.*

Classic Vinegar

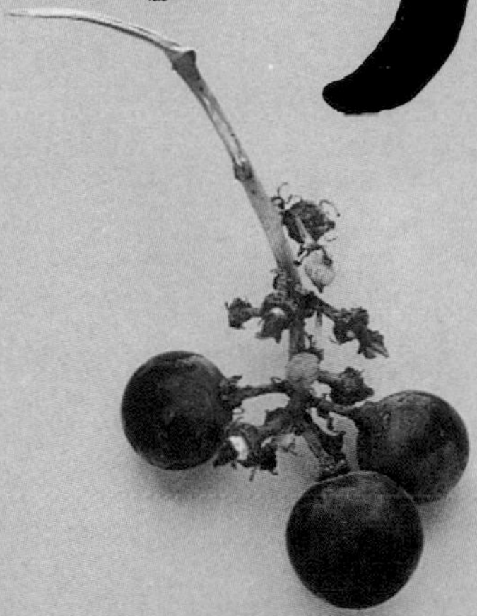

The first vinegar may, or may not, have been made from wine, but wine gave vinegar its name: from the French *vin* (wine) and *aigre* (sour). While apple cider vinegar may be the most frequently used vinegar of American cooks, wine vinegar is the preferred vinegar of French and Italians. In many recipes, apple cider vinegar may be substituted for wine vinegar of any type. It will add its own fruitiness to the dish. In this chapter's recipes I have indicated where I think cider vinegar would make a positive contribution to the dish. I have devoted a separate chapter to the unique wine vinegar of central Italy, *aceto balsamico*.

Good quality wine vinegar can be expensive, a fact that does not seem to make sense since the wine is "no good." That, however, is not the case at all. The wine that forms the base material for wine vinegar gives it all of its nuances of flavor and aroma: The better the wine, the better the vinegar. But just as it would be extravagant to buy great wines to make vinegar, it would be a mistake to think you can make fine—or even passable—vinegar from wine that is disagreeable to taste. Pour it down the sink instead and chose sound wines of clean flavors and good balance. White wines should have good fruity aromas and be dry; red wines should taste smooth and rich and not overly tannic.

In addition, the best vinegar is aged, sometimes many years before sale. Red wine vinegar is often made from wines that have been barrel-aged a year or more. Once the vinegar is made, it also might be barrel-aged before bottling, and given some bottle age before commercial release. If you choose to make vinegar at home, your result will depend, as all cooking does, on the quality of ingredients you use.

A "working" crock of vinegar could be compared to a sourdough starter. Both are "alive"—contain organisms that are responsible for the characteristic flavor. These must be kept happy with regular feeding and the right storage conditions. Like sourdough starters, each person's vinegar will have its individual character. Your own vinegar allows you another way to put a personal stamp on your cooking.

I use a good deal of wine vinegar in my cooking and choose a red wine vinegar and a champagne vinegar both of which are made in France with a 7 percent acetic acid content. I also like to use Spanish sherry vinegar, a distinctive vinegar with a dry, nutty taste. White wine and champagne vinegar are especially good for vinaigrettes for lettuce and vegetable salads, while red wine vinegar suits itself to heartier meat salads and long-cooking dishes such as braises.

My mother, Antoinette, always made the vinegar for our family's use. We liked bigger, stronger tasting vinegar than was available commercially for the big salads of greens and lettuces from her garden. Because of the vinegar's strong flavor and high acetic acid content, my mother's vinaigrettes were perhaps eight parts oil to one part vinegar. She dressed a salad by coating her hands with dressing and then tossing the salad in a big bowl. Though the proportion of oil was higher, because of the stronger vinegar flavor, she used far less dressing than she would have with the standard proportions of three to one. Commercial vinegars are diluted with water to bring their acetic acid content down to 5 or 6 percent. That water dilutes the vinegar flavor and dilutes your vinaigrette, thus you have to use more dressing to properly coat the greens and to flavor them!

Making vinegar at home is a very simple process. No fancy equipment is necessary. At its most basic, all that is needed is a clean jug, a little vinegar, a piece of clean cloth, and a bottle of sound wine.

The creature responsible for turning wine or any diluted alcoholic liquid into vinegar is a bacteria of the Acetobacter genus (high-alcohol liquids—16 percent or so—will not turn into vinegar). These bacteria float freely in the air and will settle without invitation into any open container of wine and go straight to work: They "eat" alcohol and turn it into acetic acid. Actually, the bacteria oxidize the alcohol molecule by attaching an oxygen molecule to it. Since acetification is a process requiring oxygen, the base wine needs contact with fresh air and the container should be put in an airy location. The working bacteria form a whitish veil on the surface of the liquid.

Temperature, too, is a factor. Acetobacters are not fond of extremes and prefer warm to cool. They will work at temperatures below 70°F but slowly; they will also become less active at temperatures above 90°F. The bacteria are also sensitive to sulfites. Some sulfites are a by-product of the alcoholic fermentation, and more are often added to wine to retard oxidation. Most well-made wines have low sulfite contents; typically, red wines have less sulfite added than whites. Both red and white wines, if bottle-aged, will have lower sulfite contents than when first bottled. Just to be on the safe side, aerate wine before using it for vinegar: Pour it between two pitchers several times and then leave it uncovered overnight.

A greatly simplified Orleans process can be easily adapted for the home cook. There is nothing mystifying or hard about it. You can easily make all the vinegar you use and, if you start with good wine, your results will surpass just about anything you can buy. You will also have the satisfaction of knowing no leftover wine will ever go unused.

HOW TO MAKE WINE VINEGAR AT HOME

The Orleans method, named after the French town that made it famous, produces smooth, elegant wine vinegar. The Orleans process is defined by the design of the "converter," the container in which the wine turns into vinegar. It can be a barrel (a wood barrel of oak or chestnut will add a nice flavor to the vinegar) of any convenient size (probably no more than two to four quarts capacity), a specially made crock, or a food-grade plastic jug. It needs a spigot at the bottom for removing new batches of vinegar and a hole at the top for adding new wine. In addition, the container needs one or more holes placed in a horizontal row about two-thirds of the way up the container. If using a barrel, the head (the flat end) of the barrel is the easiest place to cut these. Lay the barrel on its side to mark the place for the holes. The holes should also be covered with fine mesh screening to keep out flies and bugs.

Add 2 cups wine to your vinegar converter. Add 4 cups unpasteurized vinegar. An unpasteurized vinegar is also called an "active" vinegar because it contains active acetobacters. If you cannot find unpasteurized vinegar, add the same amount of good quality vinegar and a piece of vinegar mother. The best way to get a vinegar mother is to find someone who makes a vinegar you like and ask for a piece. They will be glad to share. (See Glossary for commercial resources.)

The vinegar protects the wine from attack by undesirable microorganisms, and the vinegar mother gives acetification a jump start. Matching the color of wine and active vinegar or mother is not necessary. If one is red and one is white, your vinegar may be blush-colored but it will still have plenty of flavor.

Add another 2 cups wine at the end of a week and continue to add wine at weekly intervals until the converter is filled to just below the row of air vents.

It is important not to disturb the surface of the liquid in the converter when adding wine. To prevent disturbing the surface, fit the hole at the top of the converter with a funnel with a very long neck that reaches close to the bottom of the container (or the funnel can be attached to a length of glass tubing).

You will notice the presence of acetobacters first as greasy-looking spots on the surface of the liquid. These eventually grow and spread, becoming a gray-white veil. Acetobacters must be in contact with air to do their work. If you splash new wine into the converter, you may cause the veil to sink. It will then no longer be in contact with oxygen and the acetobacters will cease to work.

Over time, the acetobacters multiply and the veil becomes thicker. Eventually, it becomes liver-colored and slightly wrinkled. It may get so thick, it will sink of its own weight. To prevent this, Louis Pasteur invented a small raft to float on top of the working vinegar to keep the veil afloat! But it is not necessary to build a raft, another veil will form naturally. Some vinegar makers believe a sunken mother may add off-tastes to the vinegar. When the mother sinks from its own weight, it is probably time to remove and filter the contents of the converter, rinse the converter well, and start over, adding fresh wine and unpasteurized vinegar.

After a month or 6 weeks, begin tasting the vinegar by drawing off a little bit from the spigot. Once your vinegar tastes as strong as you like it, pour the vinegar through a strainer or filter into a bottle. Fill it to the top and cork it. Add the same amount of new wine to the converter. Do not use metal caps for vinegar containers! If that is all you have, line the caps with several layers of plastic wrap. It would be better to have cork or glass stoppers.

If the vinegar bottle is filled to the top and closed, it will be protected from oxygen and the acetobacters will cease to work. If you like, you can filter the vinegar through moistened and squeezed-dry coffee filters. You can also pasteurize your vinegar to protect it from any further changes. Simply heat it to a minimum of 140°F in an open, nonreactive container. Hold it at 140° and no higher than 160°F for 20 minutes. Then pour into sterilized bottles and seal with nonmetallic stoppers. Unfortunately, heating vinegar will drive off some of its delicate aromatics. It is best to draw off only as much vinegar as you will use in a month or so.

If your vinegar tastes too strong, do not panic! Add water until you get the balance you want. Testing your homemade vinegar for its exact strength is not necessary. It is simplest to judge by taste alone, perhaps by comparing your vinegar with your favorite brand. But when a vinegar of a certain strength is needed, for instance, for pickling and preserving, use a commercial vinegar of at least 5 percent or 50 grains.

Remember to feed your vinegar converter! Once you start making vinegar, you will learn a new respect for it. It is a living product. To keep the vinegar "healthy," you need to add fresh wine about once a month.

GRILLED RADICCHIO WITH ZINFANDEL SAUCE

Years ago, one of my partners in TraVigne restaurant came back from a trip raving about a dish like this one. I set to work to figure it out and it took some doing! The trick was giving the radicchio the right flavor and grilling it without it turning black. The secret was a quick poaching in a strong vinegar solution. The radicchio emerges with a bright red color and a slightly pickled flavor while remaining crunchy. It soon became a signature dish, and while it has not been on the menu in quite some time, customers still ask for it.

1	cup dry red wine (such as zinfandel)
1	medium to large shallot, minced
1½	cups chicken stock (page 20) or low-salt, canned chicken broth
1½	cups veal stock (recipe follows) or more chicken stock
1	bay leaf
1	sprig fresh thyme (optional)
6	cups water
1½	cups white wine vinegar
2	teaspoons salt
1	medium head radicchio, quartered Extra-virgin olive oil Salt and freshly ground pepper
1	tablespoon black olive paste (see Glossary)
5	medium-size fresh basil leaves
1½	tablespoons cold unsalted butter, cut into small pieces
1	tablespoon finely chopped fresh flat-leaf parsley (optional)

Bring red wine and shallots to a boil in a large, non-reactive saucepan over high heat. Boil until reduced to about 2 tablespoons. Add chicken and veal stocks, bay leaf, and thyme and continue to boil until reduced to about ½ cup. It should be almost syrupy. Skim occasionally during reduction so final sauce will be clear. Strain and set aside. (Recipe can be made ahead to this point. Cover sauce well and refrigerate up to 2 days or freeze.)

Prepare grill or preheat broiler. Combine the water, vinegar, and 2 teaspoons salt in another large nonreactive saucepan and bring to a boil over high heat. Reduce heat and let simmer. Drop in radicchio and immediately push them under the water or they will darken and turn black. Poach 2 minutes. Try to keep quarters submerged while they cook. Remove radicchio and immediately plunge into ice water to cool. Leave radicchio in the cold water until the vegetable is really cool, 1 to 2 minutes, otherwise the center may oxidize. Drain well and squeeze out water by cupping your hands around each quarter so it holds its shape. Pat dry with paper towel, if necessary.

Brush radicchio with olive oil, sprinkle with salt and pepper, and grill or broil lightly until hot and marked by the grill on all sides, 5 to 10 minutes. Make sure the grill is not too hot or the radicchio will burn before it cooks. Set aside.

Reheat sauce to a gentle simmer and add olive paste and basil. Whisk in butter. Spoon a pool of sauce in the middle of each of 4 hot plates and top with a radicchio quarter. Garnish with parsley.

Serves 4.

CHEF'S NOTES: *Heat stocks in the microwave or on the stove before adding them to the saucepan to reduce in order to speed cooking time.*

ROASTED VEAL STOCK

A rich, veal stock is terrific to have on hand, especially for winter dishes. Ask the butcher for bones and make the stock when you will be home but not necessarily in the kitchen: You could be working at your computer and have it remind you to check the stock's progress. Roast the bones well and brown the vegetables for maximum flavor. Some custom butcher shops sell stock; you might want to investigate what is available in your neighborhood.

5	pounds veal bones
2	tablespoons extra-virgin olive oil (optional)
1	large onion, cut into 1-inch chunks
2	carrots, cut into 1-inch chunks
2	stalks celery, cut into 1-inch chunks
1	cup dry red wine
10	cups cold water
1	bay leaf
10	peppercorns
5	juniper berries

Preheat oven to 450°F. Place bones in a roasting pan or baking sheet with sides and place in the oven. Roast until browned all over, about 1 hour. Make sure to stir bones occasionally so they brown evenly.

While bones are roasting, heat olive oil in a non-reactive stockpot over medium-high heat until almost smoking. (Or use some fat from the roasting bones.) Add onion, carrot, and celery and sauté over medium heat until richly browned, about 15 minutes. Add red wine and stir well, making sure to scrape up any browned bits from the sides and bottom of the pan.

Add bones and cold water and bring to a boil over high heat. Reduce heat to a simmer and add bay leaf, peppercorns, and juniper berries. Skim frequently for the first hour and continue to simmer slowly, uncovered, another 6 hours, skimming occasionally. Strain, cool, cover, and refrigerate. When fat has congealed, lift it off and discard. Cover and refrigerate or freeze.

Makes about 5 cups.

ARBORIO RICE FLOUR COATING FOR DEEP-FRIED FOODS

Use arborio rice flour coating for fried chicken and fried vegetables such as zucchini and mushrooms. Thinly sliced lemons and whole olives, especially kalamata, are also delicious deep fried.

⅓	cup arborio rice flour (see Glossary)
⅔	cup semolina (see Glossary)
1	cup all-purpose flour
	Salt and freshly ground pepper to taste

In a bowl, combine rice flour, semolina, and all-purpose flour. Season to taste with salt and pepper. Mix well. Store in a tightly sealed jar.

Makes about 2 cups coating.

CHEF'S NOTES: *I always dip foods in buttermilk before coating and deep-frying them. I drain the buttermilk by putting the food in a strainer. Then I can sprinkle the coating directly on the food in the strainer and shake to remove excess easily.*

CRISPY SEAFOOD WITH MUSTARD SEED VINEGAR

We make this dish at TraVigne with Monterey spot prawns. It is also a good recipe for rock shrimp and other kinds of seafood, such as catfish cut into 1½-inch pieces. Use any leftover sauce as a sandwich spread on its own or mixed with mayonnaise. The sauce is delicious with rich meats such as oxtail, as well. For carefree frying, I recommend investing in an electric deep-fryer. I use only peanut oil for deep-frying, as I prefer its flavor to other possible choices. After making the recipe, fry a small potato or a handful of frozen potatoes to remove the seafood taste from the oil.

MUSTARD SEED VINEGAR SAUCE

1½	teaspoons black mustard seeds
2	tablespoons Dijon mustard
½	cup hot sweet mustard (see Chef's Notes)
¼	cup champagne vinegar or apple cider vinegar
1	teaspoon minced shallots
¼	teaspoon salt
	Pinch freshly ground pepper

DEEP-FRIED SHRIMP

4	cups peanut oil for deep-frying
1	pound rock shrimp
1	cup buttermilk
1	cup Arborio Rice Flour Coating (see previous page)

FOR THE SAUCE: Place mustard seeds in a small, heavy skillet over medium-high heat. Cook just until seeds begin to jump and pop. Immediately remove from heat and pour seeds into a small bowl to cool.

Combine remaining sauce ingredients in a blender and process until smooth. Add mustard seeds and blend briefly. Pour into a bowl or glass jar with a nonmetallic lid. Reserve until needed. Will keep, tightly covered and refrigerated, almost indefinitely.

FOR THE SHRIMP: Heat oil in a deep-fryer or a heavy, deep saucepan to 375°F. Put shrimp in a nonreactive bowl and pour buttermilk over them. Toss well.

Working in small batches, drain shrimp well in a strainer and sprinkle with arborio rice flour coating. Shake off excess and deep fry shrimp in small batches until golden brown and cooked through, about 2 minutes. To ensure a crisp result, make sure the oil temperature stays at 350° to 375° and fry in small batches. Do not poke shrimp as they cook or you will tear the coating. As each batch is cooked, drain on paper towels and season with salt and pepper. Keep warm.

Pour 1 to 2 tablespoons mustard seed vinegar on each of 6 warm plates or pour onto a platter. Divide shrimp among plates and serve immediately.

Serves 6; makes about ¾ cup mustard seed vinegar sauce.

CHEF'S NOTES: *The flavor of hot sweet mustards varies from brand to brand. I used Napa Valley Mustard Company Hot Sweet Mustard. (The Napa Valley Mustard Company is a sister brand to my Consorzio brand. Both are part of the specialty foods production and marketing company, Napa Valley Kitchens, of which I am the culinary director and a partner.) If you use a different mustard, taste the sauce for balance. It should taste slightly sweet, a little spicy, and a bit tart: the sweetness underscores the sweetness of the seafood, the spice perks up the taste buds, and the crispness of the vinegar cuts the heaviness of deep frying.*

Hearty greens, such as spinach, kale, and chard, are often simply cooked and served with vinegar. This spinach salad derives from that traditional idea. The bacon adds depth of flavor, however, to keep the cholesterol count down, I suggest making the dressing with extra-virgin olive oil. The purpose of the oven-dried fruit technique is to intensify flavor. The technique can be applied to many fruits including pears, apples, grapes, persimmons, figs, and tomatoes. Experiment with other fruits as well. The low oven temperature is important so that the fruit dries but does not really "cook." The more moist the fruit, the longer the drying will take. A convection oven works particularly well but the method works in all ovens that can maintain an even, low temperature.

OVEN-DRIED FRUIT

2	tablespoons unsalted butter
1	bay leaf
½	tablespoon balsamic vinegar
½	tablespoon freshly squeezed lemon juice
1	dozen fresh figs, halved; or 2 ripe pears, cored and sliced ¼ inch thick; or 2 cups fresh grapes
	Salt and freshly ground pepper

SALAD

1	tablespoon unsalted butter
8	pieces good crusty bread, crusts removed, and cut into ¾ x 2-inch strips
	Salt and freshly ground pepper
¼	pound bacon, cut into ½-inch pieces
3	tablespoons extra-virgin olive oil or flavored olive oil such as porcini or roasted garlic (see Glossary)
2	tablespoons finely sliced garlic
½	tablespoon finely chopped sage or ½ teaspoon dried sage
¼	cup red wine vinegar or apple cider vinegar
½	pound baby spinach

FOR THE OVEN-DRIED FRUIT: Preheat oven to 200°F. Melt butter with bay leaf in an ovenproof, nonreactive sauté pan over medium heat until butter starts to turn brown. Remove pan from heat and let cool a few seconds. Add vinegar and lemon juice. (Stand back; the vinegar hitting the hot butter may make the pan spit at you!) Add fruit, season with salt and pepper, and toss well to coat. (If using pears or apples, spread slices on a non-reactive baking sheet after tossing with butter mixture in sauté pan.) Place pan in oven and let fruit dry until edges start to dehydrate and wrinkle, and the fruit is still moist and not too chewy, 2 to 3 hours. Check progress and turn fruit occasionally so it dries evenly. You want fruit to dry, not cook. Remove and let cool. Discard bay leaf.

FOR THE SALAD: Preheat oven to 350°F. In a small, ovenproof sauté pan, melt butter over medium heat. Add bread and toss to coat well. Season with salt and pepper. Place pan in oven and toast bread until crispy and brown, about 15 minutes. Turn pieces to make sure they brown evenly. Remove, drain on paper towels, and reserve.

Heat a large sauté pan over medium-high heat. Add bacon and cook until ¾ done. It should be crispy but still moist. Remove bacon and drain on paper towels. Drain off fat and discard.

Return pan to medium-high heat and add olive oil. Heat until almost smoking, then add garlic. Sauté quickly, moving pan off and on heat to regulate temperature, until garlic is lightly toasted, about 1 minute. Add sage and stir. Add vinegar and bring just to a boil. Remove from heat, add bacon, and stir. Adjust seasoning with salt and pepper.

Arrange spinach in a salad bowl. Tear larger leaves into pieces if necessary. Add oven-dried fruit and croutons. Pour dressing over while still warm and mix well.

Serves 4.

CHEF'S NOTES: *If you have a rack with closely spaced wires, you may place the fruit on it with a pan below to catch drips. Increased air circulation will allow the fruit to dry more quickly. A convection oven would also allow faster drying.*

This is just an incredibly good dish. Smoking gives the lentils a very meaty character, almost as if the all-vegetable stew includes sausages. I came up with the idea of smoking lentils when I was composing a vegetarian menu to match a set of wonderful red wines. When we make this dish at Tra Vigne, we use three kinds of lentils: Moroccan, Turkish, and French. Because they have different cooking times, we cook them separately, then mix them together before smoking them. If you have time, you might want to experiment with different lentils as well. Though it sounds time-consuming to smoke tiny things like lentils, it takes just fifteen minutes in a covered grill. I like to serve the stew by itself, or as a bed for roasted cod, or with sausage. I even thin it with oil and vinegar to use as a warm vinaigrette for Belgian endive and asparagus.

	Large handful soaked wood chips for smoking in barbeque (see Chef's Notes)
4	tablespoons extra virgin olive oil
1	tablespoon finely chopped garlic
1	large onion, cut into ¼-inch dice
1	carrot, cut into ¼-inch dice
1	stalk celery, cut into ¼-inch dice
1	tablespoon finely chopped fresh thyme
1	bay leaf
4	cups chicken stock (page 20) or low-salt, canned chicken broth
½	pound dried green lentils Salt and freshly ground pepper
1	cup shelled, raw, shelling peas and/or beans such as English green peas, limas, or favas (about 1 pound in shells)
2	tablespoons or more sherry vinegar
2	tablespoons or more finely chopped fresh flat-leaf parsley

Prepare grill and soak wood chips for smoking. Heat 2 tablespoons olive oil in a saucepan over medium-high heat until almost smoking. Add garlic and sauté until light brown, moving the pan off and on the heat to regulate temperature. Add onion, carrot, and celery and sauté about 2 minutes. Lower heat to medium and cook until vegetables are soft, about 10 minutes. Add thyme and bay leaf. Add 2½ cups stock, bring to a boil, add lentils, 1 teaspoon salt, and ¼ teaspoon pepper. Lower heat to a simmer, cover, and cook until lentils are about half done, about 15 minutes. Add more stock if necessary.

Spread lentils and their cooking liquid on a heavy baking sheet with sides. Add soaked chips to coals, put uncovered baking sheet on grill, and cover barbeque with its lid. Smoke about 15 minutes. (Recipe can be done a day ahead to this point.) Pour lentils into a bowl, cover, and refrigerate. (The smoked flavor will intensify and distribute evenly through the lentils if allowed to rest overnight. However, the result will also be delicious if you proceed straight ahead.)

Put lentils in a deep saucepan and add shelling peas or beans. Add another ¾ to 1 cup stock. The texture should be stewlike. Bring to a boil and simmer until vegetables are tender, about 5 minutes. Remove and discard bay leaf. Add 2 tablespoons vinegar, remaining 2 tablespoons oil, and taste for seasoning. Adjust with salt, pepper, and more vinegar if necessary. Sprinkle parsley over each serving.

Serves 4.

CHEF'S NOTES: *You may use frozen peas and limas instead of fresh, just be careful not to overcook them. Other substitutions would include peeled and chopped tomatoes, roasted red peppers, or even peeled and chopped apples or pears.*

If you like a strong smoked flavor, cook the lentils a little less on the stove and smoke them longer. If you prefer just a hint of smoked flavor, cook lentils longer on the stove and cut smoking time.

The wood used for smoking adds its own flavor. Oak is always good, as is apple. But in a pinch, I have used soaked kindling. Whatever wood you use must not be treated with chemicals.

PICKLED SHRIMP
AND VEGETABLE SALAD

Use your imagination when choosing vegetables for this dish. Some suggestions include carrots, garlic cloves, mushrooms, red onions, fennel, and bell peppers. Remember to look for contrast in flavor, color, and texture and utilize produce that is in season. The salad should be lightly dressed and the dressing taste only lightly acidic because the vegetables will already taste "bright" from the pickling. Feel free to double the salad ingredients and cook them in the same amount of pickling liquid specified here. In that case, you may want to cook in batches to make sure the liquid is hot enough to cook all the ingredients evenly.

4	cups water
1	cup champagne vinegar or apple cider vinegar
1½	cups dry white wine
2	tablespoons kosher salt
½	tablespoon white peppercorns
2	tablespoons pickling spice
1	lemon, cut in half
1	bay leaf
½	cup finely chopped onion
¼	cup finely chopped carrot
¼	cup finely chopped celery
4	cups mixed vegetables for pickling (such as carrots, red onion, fennel, sweet peppers, celery, celery root, and fresh or dried and rehydrated domestic or wild mushrooms such as shiitake)
1	pound large shrimp (size 16/20 or larger), shell on

GARLIC VINAIGRETTE

¼	cup roasted garlic vinegar (page 37)
¼	cup regular olive oil or Spanish or French extra-virgin olive oil
1	tablespoon minced shallots Salt and freshly ground pepper
2	tablespoons finely chopped fresh flat-leaf parsley
4–6	large leaves Bibb or butter lettuce

In a large nonreactive stockpot, put the water, vinegar, white wine, kosher salt, peppercorns, pickling spice, lemon, bay leaf, and finely chopped onion, carrot, and celery. Bring to a boil over high heat, reduce to a simmer, and cook 3 minutes. Strain, discard vegetables and spices, and return liquid to a boil.

Cut all the vegetables to be pickled into ½-inch pieces. Slice mushrooms about ¼ inch thick. Cook each vegetable separately in the simmering pickling liquid until tender but still firm. None will take longer than about 3 minutes. Remove and spread out on a baking sheet to cool.

Bring pickling liquid to a boil again and add shrimp. Immediately remove pot from heat and let shrimp sit until done, about 3 minutes (see Chef's Notes). Remove and let cool, then peel and devein. Butterfly shrimp by cutting almost all the way through their backs up to half their length. Discard pickling liquid.

In a small bowl, whisk together the roasted garlic vinegar, olive oil, shallots, and salt and pepper to taste. Put the pickled vegetables, shrimp, and parsley in another bowl and coat lightly with dressing. To serve, place a lettuce leaf in the center of each plate. Arrange shrimp in a circle around the lettuce leaf, standing them on their spread-out butterflied tails. Mound vegetables in the center.

Serves 4 to 6.

CHEF'S NOTES: *Shrimp toughen easily when cooked at too high a heat. This technique of dropping them in boiling liquid and then immediately removing the pot from the heat results in very tender shrimp.*

Variation with Roasted Garlic Oil: You can make a dressing with ½ cup roasted garlic oil and 2 tablespoons champagne vinegar or apple cider vinegar instead of the roasted garlic vinegar and olive oil. If you have neither roasted garlic vinegar nor oil, use the same quantity of Spanish or French extra-virgin olive oil (these have a lighter taste than oils from Italy and California). Add champagne vinegar or apple cider vinegar, shallots, salt, pepper, and a tablespoon or two of roasted garlic paste. If you only have fresh garlic, use a tablespoon but cook first in olive oil until light brown.

73

Rabbit is very high in protein and low in fat. It does not taste at all gamey but has a mild flavor. Neither does it taste like chicken—but like rabbit! It is also very simple to cook—lending itself to frying, roasting, baking, braising, and grilling. If all you can find is frozen rabbit, cook it anyway. You will have great results. Make two or three times the amount of rabbit sauce you will need and freeze it. Increasing the amounts only marginally increases the amount of time it takes to prepare and you can reap the benefits thereafter on the spur of the moment!

1	frying rabbit (about 2½ pounds), split in half down the back
	Salt and freshly ground pepper
6	tablespoons red wine vinegar
1	tablespoon finely chopped fresh thyme
5	tablespoons extra-virgin olive oil
1	tablespoon plus 1 teaspoon finely chopped garlic
1	large onion, finely chopped
1	carrot, finely chopped
1	stalk celery, finely chopped
2	bay leaves
2	cups dry red wine
4	cups chicken stock (page 20) or low-salt, canned chicken broth
3	ounces pancetta, diced (see Glossary)
¼–½	stick (2 to 4 tablespoons) unsalted butter
¼	pound fresh shiitake or other wild mushrooms
1	pound dried pasta (such as penne or rigatoncini)
2	tablespoons finely chopped fresh flat-leaf parsley
½	cup freshly grated Parmesan cheese

Place rabbit in a shallow, flat nonreactive dish and season well with salt and pepper. Mix together 2 tablespoons vinegar and 1 teaspoon thyme. Pour over rabbit, coating well. Cover loosely and let marinate 15 to 20 minutes.

Heat 3 tablespoons olive oil in a nonreactive deep saucepan or Dutch oven over medium-high heat until almost smoking. Add rabbit and brown on all sides. Remove to a plate. Add 1 teaspoon garlic, and onion, carrot, and celery to the pot and sauté over medium to medium-high heat until vegetables are browned, about 10 minutes. Make sure to scrape up the browned bits from the bottom and sides of the pan. Add bay leaves, remaining 4 tablespoons vinegar, and red wine. Bring to a boil and boil until reduced by half. Add stock, return to a boil, add rabbit, and simmer, covered, until rabbit is just tender, about 12 minutes.

Remove rabbit and let cool. Return cooking liquid to a boil and boil until reduced by two-thirds. Strain, skim, and reserve. Cut rabbit meat off bones into ½-inch pieces and reserve.

Place a sauté pan over medium-high heat and add pancetta. Cook until crispy and rendered of fat. Remove and drain pancetta on paper towels. Discard fat. Add remaining 2 tablespoons olive oil and 2 tablespoons butter to sauté pan and return to medium-high heat. Add mushrooms in one layer and do not move them for 1 minute. Then sauté until brown, about 5 minutes. Add remaining 1 tablespoon garlic and sauté until light brown. Add remaining 2 teaspoons thyme and reserved pancetta. Add reserved rabbit cooking liquid and cook until reduced to a thick sauce consistency. Add rabbit meat and heat through. (Recipe can be made ahead to this point and frozen.) When ready to serve, reheat sauce and stir in remaining 2 tablespoons butter, if desired.

Bring a large pot of salted water to a boil, add pasta, and cook until al dente. Drain into a large, warmed serving bowl, add rabbit sauce, parsley, and Parmesan. Toss well and serve.

Serves 4 to 6.

BRAISED SHORT RIBS OF BEEF

This is a wonderful, hearty winter dish. It takes some time to prepare but can be done ahead (and even frozen) and reheated. Serve the short ribs with a soft polenta flavored with roasted garlic and a cheese such as telemé or Parmesan. Brining gives a result that is twice as good as not brining: The meat tastes slightly sweet, the flavor is deeper, and the meat is more tender. Use the brine for any cut of beef, poultry, game, or even soft-fleshed white fish such as cod or halibut. If you want to double the recipe, you do not need to double the brine.

BASIC BRINE FOR BEEF AND POULTRY

10	cups water
2	cups kosher salt
2	cups packed dark brown sugar
10	juniper berries, optional
2	bay leaves

SHORT RIBS

4	three-bone, cross-cut beef short ribs, 1 pound each (see Chef's Notes)
¼	cup extra-virgin olive oil
1	large onion, cut into ½-inch dice
1	stalk celery, cut into ½-inch dice
1	medium carrot, cut into ½-inch dice
	Salt and freshly ground pepper
½	cup red wine vinegar or apple cider vinegar
1	cup dry red wine
3	cups chicken stock (page 20) or low-salt, canned chicken broth
2	medium vine-ripe tomatoes, peeled, seeded, and chopped
1	tablespoon finely chopped fresh oregano
1	tablespoon finely chopped fresh flat-leaf parsley

FOR THE BRINE: Bring the brine ingredients to a boil over high heat in a large pot. Stir and simmer 3 minutes. Remove from heat, let cool, cover, then refrigerate.

Put short ribs in brine and weight down with a plate so ribs are submerged. Let sit, refrigerated, up to 4 hours. Remove meat and pat dry with paper towels.

FOR THE RIBS: Preheat oven to 350°F. Heat olive oil in a large nonreactive sauté pan over medium-high heat until oil is almost smoking. Add meat, lower heat to medium, and brown on all sides, about 10 minutes. Remove ribs to a plate as they brown. Pour off all but 2 tablespoons fat and return pan to heat.

Add onion, celery, and carrot and sauté until vegetables are browned, about 10 minutes. Make sure to scrape up any browned bits from the bottom and sides of the pan. Season with salt and pepper to taste. Add vinegar and wine and bring to a boil over high heat. Boil until reduced by half. Add stock and bring to a boil again. Add ribs, scatter tomatoes over meat, cover, and braise in the preheated oven until meat is tender, about 3 hours.

When done, remove from oven and let rest, covered, 30 minutes. The meat will reabsorb cooking liquid as it cools. Remove ribs to a platter. Pour braising liquid into a narrow bowl and skim off fat, then bring to a boil in a sauté pan and cook until reduced to a sauce consistency.

To serve, reheat meat in braising liquid. Boil to reduce to a sauce consistency if necessary. Whisk in oregano and adjust salt and pepper. Garnish with parsley.

Serves 4.

CHEF'S NOTES: *It is important to let the brine cool before adding meat, fish, or poultry. If you do not brine the meat, season it well with salt and pepper before browning. Cross-cut ribs are large, and the meat texture is dense because the cut is across the grain of the meat and the bone. They are an even size, end to end, so they soak up brine and cook at an even rate. English-cut short ribs are cut along the length of the bone. The meat tapers in thickness down toward each end and the grain is looser since it runs parallel with the bone. These short ribs will work very well as a substitute but cut the brining time to about 3 hours.*

SPICED, ROASTED CHICKEN
WITH ARUGULA

Centuries ago the spice route extended from the Far East through Africa and up through Sicily to Milan and then to Europe. Many of the spices in this recipe were used as legal tender along the route. To use them all so generously in ancient times would have been a lavish display of wealth. The spice mixture gives a complex, spicy-hot flavor to the chicken. Make enough of the mixture to keep in a jar by the stove and add it to all sorts of dishes for an extra amp of flavor. The spice mixture is also good rubbed into all types of poultry and rich fish such as tuna, salmon, mackerel, and sardines. Grinding fresh or toasted whole spices makes a big difference in your cooking. If you have enough time, make the basic brine on page 75 and brine the chicken up to an hour before coating it with spices. The chicken may be roasted, without added fat.

SPICE MIXTURE

¼	cup fennel seed
1	tablespoon coriander seeds
1	tablespoon New Mexican red pepper flakes (see Glossary)
¼	cup (1 ounce) pure California chili powder (see Glossary)
1	tablespoon white peppercorns
1	tablespoon black peppercorns
2	tablespoons kosher salt
2	tablespoons ground cinnamon

CHICKEN

1	whole chicken (about 3 pounds), cut in half down the back
3	tablespoons unsalted butter
3	cups chicken stock (page 20) or low-salt, canned chicken broth
2	tablespoons sherry vinegar
2	tablespoons finely chopped, fresh flat-leaf parsley
1	large bunch arugula

FOR THE SPICE MIXTURE: Put fennel and coriander seeds in a small dry pan and place over medium-high heat just until they begin to brown and smoke, about 1 minute. Immediately pour seeds into a bowl to cool.

Pour seeds, red pepper flakes, chili powder, and white and black peppercorns into a blender and grind until fine. Add kosher salt and cinnamon and blend again. You may have to remove the blender jar from the base and shake it occasionally to get the spices to grind evenly. If the blades stick, pour the spices through a sieve and put the larger pieces back in the blender. A coffee grinder used only for spices is particularly well suited to this job.

FOR THE CHICKEN: Lay chicken, skin side up, in a non-reactive pan and rub about 3 tablespoons spice mixture all over chicken. (If you have brined the chicken, drain it and pat dry with paper towels.) You should have an even coating on all sides. Cover and refrigerate 1 hour or longer (but no more than 24 hours). The moisture in the chicken will turn the spice coating into a crust.

Preheat oven to 450°F. Melt butter in a pan large enough to hold the chicken in one layer over medium heat. Arrange chicken in pan and place in oven. Roast until chicken is done, about 20 minutes. Baste several times with the butter in the pan.

While chicken is roasting, bring chicken stock to a boil in a saucepan and boil until reduced by half. When chicken is done, remove to a platter and keep warm. Pour off half the fat in the roasting pan and add reduced stock. Stir well to scrape up all the browned bits on bottom of pan. Place over medium-high heat and reduce almost to a syrup, about 5 minutes. Whisk in vinegar, parsley, and taste for seasoning. Set aside.

Carve chicken into serving pieces and divide among 4 plates. Spoon some of the pan sauce over each serving. Scrape remaining sauce in the pan over arugula in a bowl and toss well. Divide arugula among the plates and serve immediately.

Serves 4; makes about 1 cup spice mixture.

Herbal Vinegar

Vinegar flavored with herbs is hardly a new idea. Gardeners and cooks have been making them for centuries. For me, however, the problem with commercial herb vinegar is often a lack of flavor, while the problem with my garden is often too many herbs. If you, like me, are an enthusiastic grower of herbs, your tarragon grows to three feet high and so does the oregano. The question is always: What to do with it all?

Using the bounty to make strongly flavored herb vinegar is as good an answer as I can think of. The technique I use is a simple, quick purée of herbs and vinegar that is immediately strained to give a fresh and delightfully flavorful result. You can use up all your excess herbs and produce a huge flavor that you can thin out with more vinegar if you choose. Having too much flavor is not the problem, having not enough flavor is.

To use my technique, you do not have to think way ahead but can take inspiration from the moment—from whatever is at the market or in the garden. In fact, I would advise making only small batches of vinegar so that its flavor is as fresh as possible. Rose petals, lemon verbena, and sage will each make wonderful vinegar. You might try complementary flavors—blends of fruit and herb vinegar, for instance, or add sage to raspberry, and basil to mango. Or use several herbs to mix into a tomato-garlic vinegar to create a Mediterranean-inspired blend. Only be sure your herbs, vegetables, and flowers, especially, are not sprayed with any pesticides!

Various herbal vinegars are wonderful additions to the pantry if only because we eat so many salads these days. Making vinaigrette with a different vinegar each time can vary the flavor without having to create a whole new recipe. Herbal vinegar can also perk up and add new flavors to all sorts of sauces and soups, especially tomato- and bean-based preparations.

The one herb I would not recommend infusing is thyme. I use a good deal of thyme in my cooking and always use the fresh herb. Its flavor is not appealing to me either dried or infused in vinegar or oil. I recommend growing thyme in your garden or in a pot in a sunny location even if you grow no other herbs. Luckily, fresh herbs are becoming more common in supermarkets and, because thyme is so widely used, it should be available fresh year-round.

Make herbal vinegars with good quality champagne vinegar. The flavor of red wine vinegar will mask that of most herbs. Rosemary, however, makes a very good flavored red wine vinegar. Use red wine vinegar to make assertive spice vinegars or lively blends of herbs and spices such as bay, garlic, black pepper, and rosemary. How much of each ingredient you use to flavor the vinegar depends on your taste as well as the quality of the ingredients to be infused. Start with more rather than less and search for the most flavorful herbs and freshest spices you can find. If the result is too strong, add unflavored vinegar until you have a balance you like.

If you want to infuse spices such as peppercorns, coriander, juniper, and the like, heat the vinegar to just under boiling. Add spices and let sit until cool. Do not strain out spices before bottling. To make an interesting chili vinegar, infuse peppercorns and dried chilies in hot vinegar, then bottle with chopped fresh hot and sweet peppers.

Use herbal vinegars in any recipe calling for white wine vinegar or champagne vinegar. The herbal flavor will increase the complexity of the dish.

As with all vinegars, use nonreactive cookware when heating them, store them in glass containers, and do not use metallic caps or lids to cover them.

BASIC PROCEDURE FOR MAKING HERBAL VINEGAR

This is an incredibly simple, fast process that gives a fresh herb flavor. Your base vinegar takes on just a tinge of color, which, however, is not stable: The fresh, light green begins to oxidize in a few minutes and takes on a slight brownish cast in comparison to when first made. For the most spectacular presentation, make the vinegar just before use. The flavor does not change even if the color does. Add a leaf or two of the fresh herb to the bottle when bottling to help with identification.

I use vinegar with six percent acidity for these herbal vinegars, the standard strength of many imported vinegars. The American vinegar standard is usually five percent. If you use a stronger vinegar, increase the amount of fresh herbs. When you use your herbal vinegar in other recipes, you will have to taste as you go and adjust for a balance that suits your palate.

I suggest straining herb vinegar through a fine mesh sieve. If you want a very clear vinegar, you can filter it through rinsed and squeezed-dry coffee filters. However, you will also be filtering out flavor.

A very pretty touch is to add the herb flowers to the vinegar once it is strained, especially chive blossoms, separated into florets. These have a wonderful, zesty bite to them and it is a shame to see them dry and unpicked on the plant.

1   cup fresh green herb leaves,
       tightly packed (such as basil, tarragon,
       lavender flowers and leaves, oregano,
       mint, sage, chives)
1   cup champagne vinegar (6 percent acidity)
       Pinch salt

Put herbs, vinegar, and salt in a blender and blend on high speed about 30 seconds. Strain through a fine strainer into a clean, glass bottle. Press on the solids to extract all the vinegar and flavor. Use immediately when it is a fresh, frothy, delicate green. The color will oxidize right before your eyes, turning darker green with a brownish hue. The flavor, however, is stable. Store the vinegar in a cool, dark place, tightly covered with a nonmetallic lid.

Makes about 1 cup.

CHEF'S NOTES: *Opal basil keeps its lovely opal color and allows you surprising presentation possibilities.*

Variation for Rosemary Vinegar: Use ½ cup rosemary sprigs to 1 cup vinegar. Also, in winter or under drought conditions, rosemary will get very tough and resinous. If this is the shape your rosemary is in, blanch it first for about 30 seconds in boiling water. It is not necessary to plunge it in ice water afterwards, just put it straight into the blender with the vinegar.

MIGNONETTE
WITH JET COLD OYSTERS

Here in northern California we are lucky to have terrific oyster farmers. Many people make an outing of driving to Bodega Bay or Inverness in order to stop for oysters and see the ocean. The oystermen also often come inland to our farmers' markets. Oysters can close their shells so tightly that they remain alive, if kept cold, even if out of the water for several days. This simple, traditional sauce for oysters is a wonderful way to showcase freshly made herbal vinegar. Make sure your pepper is freshly cracked. The flavor of the coarse bits of pepper are a great foil for the sweet saltiness of the oysters. Have twenty-four oysters for four romantic people.

1	shallot, finely minced
3	tablespoons herbal vinegar (page 82), flavored with tarragon
	Salt and freshly cracked pepper
1	teaspoon finely chopped fresh flat-leaf parsley
24	fresh oysters on the half shell (see Chef's Notes)

In a small bowl, mix together shallot, vinegar, and salt and pepper to taste. Add parsley just before serving. The parsley helps the mignonette adhere to the oysters. Arrange oysters, still on their half shells, on a bed of ice and spoon mignonette over them.

Serves 4 as an appetizer.

CHEF'S NOTES: *When you buy your oysters, buy them as fresh as possible. Ask the oysterman or fishmonger how old the oysters are. Do not buy them if they are more than three days old. Also, have the fishmonger shuck the oysters for you, leaving them on the half shell and catching the oyster liquor in the take-home container.*

TOD'S COLESLAW

Todney Stoner, sous chef of our restaurant, Ajax Tavern, in Aspen, Colorado, gave me his mother's family recipe for coleslaw. His family is from West Virginia and the salad is one of the most amazingly good-tasting slaws I have ever had. It is awesome on a barbecued piece of brisket. Tod makes it every day for the restaurant, varying it occasionally by adding other vegetables such as carrot and radicchio.

1	head (about 2 pounds) white cabbage, finely shredded
¾	cup finely sliced red onion
1	cup sugar
1	cup herbal vinegar (page 82) or apple cider vinegar
¾	cup vegetable oil or corn oil
1	tablespoon whole celery seed
1	teaspoon salt

Layer ⅓ of the cabbage and onion in a nonreactive bowl. Sprinkle with ¼ cup sugar. Repeat twice and let sit 15 to 20 minutes at room temperature.

Combine remaining ¼ cup sugar with vinegar, oil, celery seed, and salt in a nonreactive saucepan and bring to a boil over high heat. Stir until sugar is dissolved. Immediately pour over the cabbage and onion and mix well. Cover with plastic wrap and weight down with cans or even with a stack of plates. Refrigerate 24 hours before serving.

Serves 6 to 8.

Variation with Red Cabbage: Red cabbage makes a pretty slaw. Do not try a mix of green and red; the red color bleeds and colors the whole batch.

POACHED EGG AND PROSCIUTTO BRUSCHETTA

This makes a great brunch, lunch, or late supper dish—very easy to cook and full of satisfying flavors and textures. Though it may seem strange to dress greens with vinegar alone and to drizzle the cooked eggs with more vinegar, trust me! The acidity cuts the sometimes heavy, fat flavor of egg yolk and leaves the palate refreshed.

4	long slices crusty, country bread, cut about ½ inch thick
2	tablespoons flavored olive oil such as roasted garlic or basil olive oil (see Glossary)
8	thin slices (about 1½ ounces total) prosciutto
4	cups water
¾	cup (about) herbal vinegar (page 82), such as basil or chive
8	eggs
2–3	cups mixed salad greens
	Salt and freshly ground pepper

Lightly brush bread on one side with oil and toast on both sides. Cut each piece in half on the diagonal and put 2 halves (oiled side up) on each of 4 hot plates. Arrange a slice of prosciutto on top of each half. Keep warm.

Bring 4 cups water and ½ cup herbal vinegar to a boil in a wide nonreactive saucepan but make sure water is at least 1½ inches deep. Poach eggs by cracking them and then slipping them gently into the water. Use a spoon to hold the whites close to the yolk. Poach just a few at a time and cook just until whites are set and yolks are still runny, about 1½ minutes. Remove and drain on paper towels.

Season greens with salt and pepper and a splash of vinegar. Arrange a handful on each plate, then top each piece of toast with an egg and season with salt and pepper. Drizzle or spray a little more vinegar over the eggs and serve.

Serves 4.

I find it nearly impossible to get flavor in cold pasta salads; the starch seems to hide all my flavor efforts. This warm pasta salad has a clean, light taste. The sauce is a pan vinaigrette. It and the vegetables may be done ahead of time, but the pasta should be cooked at the last minute so it is hot when mixed with the vinaigrette. The dish is then served warm or at room temperature. Feel free to use any vegetables you like—for instance, asparagus and roasted red bell peppers—taking advantage of seasonal produce.

1	pound broccoli
5	tablespoons extra-virgin olive oil
2	tablespoons finely chopped garlic
¼	teaspoon New Mexican red pepper flakes (see Glossary)
1	tablespoon finely chopped fresh thyme
	Salt and freshly ground pepper
2	cups chicken stock (page 20) or low-salt canned chicken broth
1	pound zucchini, sliced into ¼-inch-thick rounds (if large, cut zucchini in half first)
3	tablespoons herbal vinegar (page 82), flavored with oregano
2	medium tomatoes, cut into large chunks
2	tablespoons finely chopped fresh flat-leaf parsley
1	pound dried fusilli pasta
½	cup freshly grated Parmesan cheese

Separate broccoli into florets. Peel stems down to the light green, tender core, then slice into thin rounds on the diagonal. Keep florets and stems separate.

Heat 2 tablespoons oil in a sauté pan until almost smoking. Add garlic and sauté until light brown, moving the pan off and on heat to regulate temperature. Add red pepper flakes and thyme. Stir. Add broccoli florets and sauté about 1 minute. Season with salt and pepper.

Add chicken stock to sauté pan and bring to a boil. Cook until broccoli is half cooked, about 3 minutes. Add broccoli stems and zucchini and cook until tender, about another 3 minutes. Dip out vegetables with a strainer and spread on a baking sheet to cool.

Bring cooking liquid to a boil and boil until it is thick and saucelike. You should have about ½ cup. Add vinegar, stir, then add tomatoes and stir just so they warm but do not cook. Season to taste with salt and pepper. Add remaining olive oil and parsley. Mix well.

Meanwhile, bring a large pot of salted water to a boil. Cook pasta until al dente, drain, pour into a serving bowl, and immediately toss with pan vinaigrette, vegetables, and half the cheese. Sprinkle with remaining cheese and serve warm.

Serves 4 to 6.

This is not a California Cuisine salad! When I braise vegetables, I like them to be meltingly tender at the finish. This is when their flavor is the sweetest. I have created a fun presentation for a very earthy salad but since taste is more important, feel free to cut the vegetables into bite-size pieces and toss with the dressing in a serving bowl. The tops and trimmings from the leeks may be fried for a garnish or saved for making soup.

4	medium potatoes (about 1 pound), such as Yukon Gold or red potatoes
1	pound trimmed leeks (about ¾ inch in diameter or larger leeks cut in half)
2	tablespoons unsalted butter
1	bay leaf
1	tablespoon finely chopped fresh thyme Salt and freshly ground pepper
1	cup chicken stock (page 20) or low-salt canned chicken broth
2	tablespoons herbal vinegar (page 82), flavored with chives
1	tablespoon finely chopped fresh flat-leaf parsley
2	tablespoons extra-virgin olive oil
1	tablespoon finely chopped fresh chives Fried julienne of leek, optional (see Chef's Notes)

Put unpeeled potatoes in a pot of salted, cold water and bring to a boil. Simmer until tender, about 15 minutes. Do not overcook. Drain, let cool, and cut into ⅜-inch-thick slices. Keep slices in order so potatoes may be reassembled.

Preheat oven to 350°F. Cut off and discard all but 5 or 6 inches of white parts of leeks. Melt butter with bay leaf in an ovenproof skillet over medium-high heat. Add white parts of leeks and toss to coat well with butter. Add thyme and season with salt and pepper. Add chicken stock and bring to a boil. Cover and cook in the preheated oven until very tender, about 20 minutes. When done, drain leeks and let cool on a plate. Remove and discard bay leaf from skillet, but do not discard cooking liquid. Cut leeks lengthwise into halves or quarters, if necessary. Season again with salt and pepper.

Place skillet with cooking liquid over medium-high heat. Bring to a boil and boil until reduced to a sauce consistency, about ¼ cup. Remove from heat and immediately whisk in 1½ tablespoons vinegar. Add parsley. Slowly add olive oil while whisking to form an emulsion. Taste for balance and add more vinegar if necessary.

Arrange about 3 pieces of leek on each of 4 plates. Drizzle with pan vinaigrette. Lay potato slices out in order, season with salt and pepper, and drizzle with vinaigrette. Turn over and repeat on the second side. Stack potato slices on each plate to reassemble one potato per person. Drizzle with more vinaigrette and sprinkle with chives. Garnish the top with a small handful of fried leeks, if desired.

Serves 4.

CHEF'S NOTES: *Fried leek tops are delicious and a good use of some of the leek tops that might otherwise be thrown away. They make a nice complement to fish dishes as well as this salad. Cut the pale, yellow-green inner leaves lengthwise into strips as fine as you can manage. Dip in buttermilk, drain, then toss with arborio rice flour coating (page 68). Deep-fry in 375°F oil until crispy and a pale gold.*

It is important to start potatoes cooking in cold water so they will cook evenly throughout.

TOMATO AND GORGONZOLA SALAD
WITH CRISPY ONION RINGS

The cheese and onion rings provide enough fat so that a vinaigrette with oil is unnecessary. I do recommend buying a deep-fat fryer if you like to make fried foods with any regularity. The fryer keeps temperatures even and, because the heating coils are on the sides as opposed to the bottom, the solids that always fall to the bottom of the pan will not burn and spoil the flavor of the oil and the food you are preparing.

4	cups peanut oil for deep-frying
1	red onion, sliced ⅜ inch thick and separated into rings (see Chef's Notes)
½	cup buttermilk
½	cup seasoned arborio rice flour coating (page 68) Salt and freshly ground pepper
2	pounds (about 4 large) vine-ripe tomatoes
⅓	cup finely crumbled Gorgonzola or other blue-veined cheese or freshly grated Parmesan cheese
2	tablespoons herbal vinegar (page 82), flavored with basil or oregano

In a deep-fat fryer or large heavy saucepan, heat oil to 375°F (see Chef's Notes). Preheat oven to 200°F. Place onions in a nonreactive bowl and pour buttermilk over them. Toss well. Place onions in a strainer to drain well, then dust with rice flour coating. Shake off excess over a plate or waxed paper. Deep-fry until golden brown, about 2 minutes. Do not touch the onions too often or you will rip the coating. Keep them separate and try to keep them under the surface of the fat so they brown evenly. The first batch will cook more quickly than the remainder. Drain on paper towels, sprinkle with salt, and place in oven to keep warm. Onions can be made ahead and kept warm; this coating does not get soggy.

Cut a slice off the top and bottom of each tomato (do not core) and cut in half horizontally. Arrange tomatoes on a platter or 2 slices on each of 4 plates. Season with salt and pepper and sprinkle with cheese and vinegar. Top each salad with about 3 overlapping onion rings and serve.

Serves 4.

CHEF'S NOTES: *Use the larger, outer rings for this dish and save the smaller, inner rings for another purpose.*

For the best frying results, as I have said, I recommend a deep-fryer. Second best is to have a deep-frying thermometer because temperature is so important. You want the food to cook quickly and to get brown and crisp without burning (temperature is too hot) and without getting soggy (temperature is too low). If, however, you have neither deep-fryer nor thermometer, heat your oil over medium-high heat until you can see it begin to swirl. Begin to test the temperature by dropping in a single piece of food, such as a frozen French fry. The oil will be hot enough when it actively bubbles as soon as the potato is put in and the potato browns crisply within about 1 minute. Make sure to bring the oil temperature back up to the correct heat between batches.

ARBORIO RICE FLOUR: *My staff and I worked a long time to find a perfect coating for fried foods. One day we tested every flour we had, in every combination. It occurred to me to use the rice powder mixed with flour as a coating for fried foods. Rice has a higher sugar content than wheat so it would brown more quickly in the fryer. The seafood would not overcook before the coating browned. In addition, the slightly grainy texture of the rice "flour" makes the coating attractive to the eye as well as the tooth and, even better, it does not get soggy! This allows the cook to make the fried food ahead of time and keep it warm in a low oven! I use arborio rice to make my rice flour because Tra Vigne is an Italian restaurant. However, you can use any white rice. You will need to blend at least a cup at a time. Place rice in blender and blend until you have tiny granules about the texture of powdered gelatin. One cup rice yields a little less than 1¼ cups rice flour. For my rice flour coating for deep-frying, see page 68.*

CALIFORNIA CHILI POWDER: *This is not like the chili powder found in the spice section of grocery stores. Those are most commonly a blend of powdered chilies, cumin, and oregano. California chili powder is finely ground, whole, dried California chilies with nothing added. California chilies are only mildly hot. You can find whole and ground California chilies in well-stocked Mexican groceries. Two brands are Mojave Foods (6200 E. Slauson Avenue, City of Commerce, CA 90040) and El Guapo (631 S. Anderson Street, Los Angeles, CA 90023). Also look for various types of dried chilies at your farmers' market. Tierra Vegetables grows many varieties of chilies without pesticides, herbicides, or fumigants. You can mail order their dried chilies. Write to them at 13684 Chalk Hill Road, Healdsburg, CA 95448; 707-433-5666.*

FLAVORED OLIVE OIL: *My brand, Consorzio, makes several flavored oils and, in 1994, I wrote a small book about making and using flavored oils: Flavored Oils: 50 Recipes for Cooking with Infused Oils, published in 1995 by Chronicle Books. Flavored oils are easily made by briefly puréeing a large amount of fresh herbs (such as basil) with a small amount of oil, filtering the result, and "thinning" with more olive oil. The oil should not be an extra-virgin olive oil. It has too distinct a taste of its own and will compete with the flavor you want to add to the oil. To infuse spices such as cinnamon and peppercorns, dried chilies, dried, wild mushrooms, and resinous herbs such as rosemary, heat the flavoring and oil together very gently for less than a minute, then filter. Again use a large amount of spice and a small amount of oil (1 cup minimum to make it worth your while). If the flavor is too strong, just add more oil to achieve the balance you prefer.*

Roasted garlic oil, one of the most popular oils and a wonderful oil with many applications at the stove (I use it to sauté all sorts of vegetables, to add to salad dressings, and the like) is the by-product of making roasted garlic. Or roasted garlic is the by-product of roasted garlic oil! Roast six to eight large heads of fresh garlic seasoned with salt and pepper, in a cup or two of olive oil until tender, very soft, and caramelized. Use the paste to spread on toast or sandwiches, to stir into soup, and so forth, and bottle the oil.

Flavored oils will keep, refrigerated, for a week. I recommend making small batches with the most flavorful herbs and spices you can find. Taste the oil you plan to use as well to make sure it has a pleasantly neutral flavor. If you do not have the flavored oil called for in a recipe, go ahead and make it anyway. Use extra-virgin olive oil and, if you have it, the fresh herb.

For food safety reasons, it is important to make only small batches of flavored oils, keep them refrigerated, and to use them quickly, within a week. If you choose to make garlic oil, soak the raw cloves in distilled vinegar for 30 minutes, then rinse with water, drain, and pulse in a blender with a little oil. Press the oil out of the solids, discard solids, and add more oil to the flavored oil until you have a flavor balance to suit your palate.

KOSHER SALT: *I use only kosher salt in my cooking. I like the fact that it is pure salt. The table salt label in front of me lists calcium silicate, dextrose, and potassium iodide as well as salt. Kosher salt is also less expensive than sea salt. If you want to use the best salt I know of, look in specialty markets for "gray salt," an unprocessed sea salt from Brittany, France. If you do not have, or cannot find kosher salt, use table salt but in lower amounts than my recipes specify.*

NEW MEXICAN CHILI FLAKES/RED PEPPER FLAKES: *Chilies vary in heat from brand to brand. Shop until you find a brand you like, then stick with it. New Mexican chilies are medium hot. You can substitute the crushed red pepper flakes you find easily in the supermarket, but you may want to cut back on the amount called for in my recipe. You can find New Mexican chilies in well-stocked Mexican groceries. Buy the whole, dried chilies and grind them coarsely. Store in a tightly sealed jar.*

OLIVE PASTE: *Olive paste is simply very finely chopped and pitted olives. It can be made from green olives though it is more commonly made from black olives. Brined olives such as kalamata give the paste a different flavor than intense, oil-cured olives. Black olive paste (usually flavored with anchovy and capers) is the base for tapenade, a typical Provençal spread served on toast as an appetizer.*

PANCETTA: *A cured, unsmoked bacon made from the fat meat of the pig's belly and seasoned with salt, pepper, and spices. It usually comes rolled and cut into thin slices. Cook it as you would bacon.*

PIZZA DOUGH: Once you have made pizza dough from scratch, you will see it is not as much effort as you might have thought. And you have the benefit of being able to make your pizza exactly the size and thickness you like best. If you prefer a thick-crusted pizza, double this recipe.

1   cake (0.6 ounce) fresh yeast
    or 1 package active dry yeast
½   cup lukewarm water
3½ cups all-purpose flour plus
    additional flour for kneading
½   cup whole wheat flour
1   cup water
2   tablespoons extra-virgin
    olive oil plus additional oil
    for brushing bowl and dough
2   teaspoons salt
    Coarse cornmeal for baking sheet

Combine yeast, the warm water, and ½ cup of the flour in the bowl of an electric mixer. Let stand 15 minutes to activate yeast. Add the remaining 3 cups all-purpose flour, whole wheat flour, the 1 cup water, olive oil, and salt. Mix with the dough hook attachment on low, then increase speed to medium-low until the dough comes away from the bottom of the bowl. Dough should be slightly moist. Knead another minute.

Turn out dough onto a lightly floured surface and knead gently until smooth, folding the dough over itself. Shape into a ball, flatten into a fat disc with the heel of your hand, and put in an oiled bowl. Cover with a damp towel and let rise in a warm place until doubled in bulk, about 1 hour. Punch down and cut into 3 equal pieces. Roll each into a ball. Dough may be frozen at this point

(see Chef's Notes). Brush lightly with olive oil and let rise in a warm place, covered, in oiled bowls or on a floured board, until doubled in size, about 30 minutes. Dough is now ready to be shaped and baked as directed in recipe.

Makes about 2 pounds dough; enough for three 10-inch pizzas.

Chef's Notes: If you freeze the pizza dough, defrost and let rise in the refrigerator. It triples and quadruples in volume with this method so be sure to use a large bowl and watch carefully that it does not overflow.

You can roll out the dough with a rolling pin but this presses all the air out of the edges and creates a very flat pizza. Toppings that are slightly liquid, such as tomato sauce, or that melt, such as mozzarella, will leak off and spill. It is better to shape the dough by hand, pulling and stretching gently. The unevenness adds to the pizza's charm.

POLENTA: Polenta (the dried ground kernels of corn) is a New World food introduced to Europe by explorers who reached the Americas. It fit well into the peasant style of cooking throughout Italy. Peasant cuisines usually include a cooked grain mush as a staple of the diet. The grain would be whatever grew well in that region. It is the Italians, however, who made an inspired dish of simple cornmeal mush. The word polenta is used for both the grain—coarsely ground, yellow cornmeal—and the dish it makes when cooked with water or other liquid into a stiff paste.

ROASTING BELL PEPPERS AND CHILI PEPPERS: Roast peppers under a broiler or over an open flame or grill, turning occasionally until skins char and blacken all over. Place in a closed bag or a bowl with a lid and allow steam to loosen skins. When cool enough to handle, peel off skins. Remove and discard core, seeds, and veins. Do not rinse the peppers as you peel them; you will wash their flavor down the drain!

When handling hot chili peppers, take care not to burn your face or eyes: wear gloves and/or wash your hands and the cutting board immediately after handling them. Do not touch your face or other sensitive parts of your body!

SEMOLINA: Semolina is produced by milling durum wheat, a hard, winter wheat. After the bran is removed and before the grains are ground into flour, large particles of the endosperm are separated out and sold separately as semolina. It is pale yellow and has a coarse texture. Semolina is used in puddings, as a thickener in soups, and to make pasta. It can be purchased in Italian food markets.

TOASTED PINE NUTS, PISTACHIOS, AND OTHER NUTS: Preheat oven to 350°F. Scatter nuts on a baking pan and place in oven until lightly browned. Stir occasionally so they brown evenly. Pine nuts should take no longer than 3 to 5 minutes and burn easily, so keep your eye on them! Pistachios take about 5 minutes; walnuts, hazelnuts, and pecans take about 10 minutes. A toaster oven

works very well for this small job. You might want to toast a larger amount than any recipe calls for, then store the extra toasted nuts in a glass jar in the freezer.

VINEGAR-MAKING SUPPLIES: The Cantinetta, our small delicatessen and take-out food shop across the stone courtyard from Tra Vigne, can fit out the new vinegar maker with whatever is needed: We carry a specially designed vinegar-making crock (it comes with a recipe for homemade vinegar) and "active" vinegar we make ourselves. You can write The Cantinetta at Tra Vigne, 1050 Charter Oak Road, St. Helena, CA 94574, or call 707-963-8888. Home winemaking shops are another good source for equipment and advice. One such is Napa Fermentation Supplies, P. O. Box 5839, Napa, CA 94581; 707-255-6372. This shop sells an 8-ounce jar of vinegar mother and provides a sheet of instructions.

TABLE OF EQUIVALENTS

The exact equivalents in the following tables have been rounded for convenience.

OVEN TEMPERATURES

Fahrenheit	Celsius	Gas
250	120	½
275	140	1
300	150	2
325	160	3
350	180	4
375	190	5
400	200	6
425	220	7
450	230	8
475	240	9
500	260	10

LIQUIDS

US	Metric	UK
2 tbl	30 ml	1 fl oz
¼ cup	60 ml	2 fl oz
⅓ cup	80 ml	3 fl oz
½ cup	125 ml	4 fl oz
⅔ cup	160 ml	5 fl oz
¾ cup	180 ml	6 fl oz
1 cup	250 ml	8 fl oz
1½ cups	375 ml	12 fl oz
2 cups	500 ml	16 fl oz
4 cups/1 qt	1 l	32 fl oz

US/UK

oz=ounce
lb=pound
in=inch
ft=foot
tbl=tablespoon
fl oz=fluid ounce
qt=quart

WEIGHTS

US/UK	Metric
1 oz	30 g
2 oz	60 g
3 oz	90 g
4 oz (¼ lb)	125 g
5 oz (⅓ lb)	155 g
6 oz	185 g
7 oz	220 g
8 oz (½ lb)	250 g
10 oz	315 g
12 oz (¾ lb)	375 g
14 oz	440 g
16 oz (1 lb)	500 g
1½ lb	750 g
2 lb	1 kg
3 lb	1.5 kg

LENGTH MEASURES

⅛ in	3 mm
¼ in	6 mm
½ in	12 mm
1 in	2.5 cm
2 in	5 cm
3 in	7.5 cm
4 in	10 cm
5 in	13 cm
6 in	15 cm
7 in	18 cm
8 in	20 cm
9 in	23 cm
10 in	25 cm
11 in	28 cm
12 in/1 ft	30 cm

METRIC

g=gram
kg=kilogram
mm=millimeter
cm=centimeter
ml=milliliter
l=liter